Mental Maths

for ages 5 to 7

Teacher's book

Anita Straker

CAMBRIDGE
UNIVERSITY PRESS

For my grandson Sam, born 1 September 1995.

Published by the Press Syndicate of the University of Cambridge
The Pitt Building, Trumpington Street, Cambridge CB2 1RP
40 West 20th Street, New York, NY 10011-4211, USA
10 Stamford Road, Oakleigh, Melbourne 3166, Australia

© Cambridge University Press 1996

First published 1996

Printed in Great Britain by Scotprint Ltd, Musselburgh

Cover illustration by Tony Hall
Cartoons by Tim Sell

A catalogue record for this book is available from the British Library

ISBN   0 521 57764 0

Introduction

This series is intended to help children think about numbers and carry out mental calculations. There are three teacher's books and seven booklets of short exercises for pupils: one teacher's book and one booklet for children aged 5 to 7, a second teacher's book and two more booklets for ages 7 to 9, and a third teacher's book and three more booklets for ages 9 to 11. The final pupil's booklet is mainly for lower secondary pupils.

Mental Maths for ages 5 to 7 is the first teacher's book. It contains ideas for you to work on with groups of children or a whole class and photocopiable pages of puzzles and games for children to do by themselves. *Mental Maths Starter Book* is published separately and is intended for six- to seven-year-olds to work from, either at school or at home.

Part 1: Ways of working   **Page 2**

Part 1 of this book contains brief advice on things like classroom organisation and ways in which children can record their answers. It stresses the importance of counting activities and the value of discussing children's methods.

Part 2: Oral work   **Page 9**

Part 2 has a series of suggestions for oral work at national curriculum levels 1 to 3. Each activity is designed to be led by a teacher or classroom assistant and will last for up to 10 minutes. The level of difficulty is indicated for each one. Several of the activities are suitable for a whole class to work on together, since questions and responses are possible at more than one level. Others are more suitable for a small group working at roughly the same level. In Part 2a, the equipment needed, the vocabulary to emphasise and the questions to ask are described in detail. In Part 2b, ideas are described more briefly.

Part 3: Puzzles and games   **Page 47**

Part 3 consists of photocopiable pages of puzzles or games for children to work on by themselves. The puzzles are for individual children to do, either in school or at home. The games are intended for two or more children to play together. Some older infants may be able to read the instructions or the rules for themselves but younger or less confident readers may need some help in order to get started. In most cases children will be able to complete the activity in about 10 to 15 minutes. Levels of difficulty for each activity, and solutions to the puzzles, are given on pages 72 to 74.

Answers: *Mental Maths Starter Book*   **Page 75**

Answers to the questions in the separately published *Mental Maths Starter Book* are given on pages 75 to 78 of this book. They are also in the *Answer Book* which accompanies the whole series. The *Starter Book* contains exercises and puzzles at levels 2 or 3 of the national curriculum and is a first mental maths book for children aged 6 upwards. Less confident children may need some help with drawing some of the diagrams.

Part 1: Ways of working

Mental work with numbers

All teachers know that mental arithmetic is important and that children need lots of varied opportunities to practise. Five minutes of 'carpet time' each day to talk about mathematics is preferable to half-an-hour once a week. A session can be fitted at the start or end of a day, or between two other activities, or at any time when the context provides an opportunity to talk about any aspect of mathematics.

You can also use your five-minute sessions to:

- revise last week's number work;
- ask questions related to classroom displays;
- help children to use and apply mathematics to investigate or solve problems;
- extend their mathematical vocabulary;
- assess the skills of individual children.

Organising the class

To achieve the right atmosphere for thinking, you will need to establish the way that you want to work with the children. For example, you might say:

- Today we are going to think about numbers. We won't be using pencil and paper or calculators or fingers to help work things out – we will just use our heads.
- When you are thinking, it sometimes helps to shut your eyes.
- Try not to interrupt when anyone else is speaking.
- If you have something to say, or are ready to tell me your answer, don't call out as it might distract someone who is still thinking.

Organising groups

Research suggests that groups do better where children of high and middle ability work together, and children of middle and lower ability. As far as you can, try to have equal numbers of girls and boys in each group.

If the groups are to be left to work on their own for a while, you may want to spend more time with one particular group, asking questions, observing and giving feedback, directing suitable questions to individuals and encouraging the more reluctant.

In the other groups there is always the danger that without the presence of an adult some children may dominate and others may just sit quietly. All children are more likely to learn if they have an active part to play. Some roles you could give them are:

- a starter: who makes sure that everyone understands what is to be done and who calls you if the group gets stuck;
- an organiser: who collects the things that are needed for the activity, gives them out to everyone in the group, and gathers them together at the end;
- a reader: who helps anyone who doesn't understand any difficult words;
- a time-keeper: who starts and stops the clock for any timed activities;
- a referee: who makes sure that turns are taken fairly and that everyone has an equal chance to contribute;
- a recorder: who has pencil and paper to note any scores;
- a reporter: who agrees with the group what will be reported to you or to the whole class at the end of the activity.

Recording answers in oral work

Most of the answers to your questions will be given orally. This helps to build children's confidence and speed without the need for any formal recording.

With larger groups it is more difficult to involve everyone if all the answers are spoken. There are various strategies for recording which help to ensure that each child responds.

- Answers up to 10 (or 20) can be recorded on individual number strips. Start each question by saying something like: 'Colour this number blue'. At the end of your questions you can check their answers by asking: 'Which number did you colour blue?' Children can also compare their patterns of colours to identify any errors.

- Another way is to give each member of the group a pack of number cards. Children simply pick from their packs the card which corresponds to their answer and put it in front of them on the table top. Alternatively, they can hold it up to show you.

- With two-digit answers, you can use sets of double width cards for numerals 10 to 90, and single width for 1 to 9. When you ask a question, each child places the appropriate units card on top of the tens card, and holds it on the table top while you check their responses. This also helps to reinforce place value.

- As an alternative, provide them with a 100-square. As questions are asked, numbers corresponding to answers can be covered with a counter or coloured on the square. It is easy for you to walk round the class and see who has covered what.

- Older children can, of course, write their answers on a piece of paper.

Discussing the methods used

Methods of mental arithmetic are based on a sound understanding of place value together with good recall of number facts. Your aim is to build up children's speed and confidence in recalling facts, and their awareness of the number system, without worrying about formal recording. It can help to repeat a 'fact of the day' in as many voices as possible: shout it, sing it, say it in a rumbling voice, use a piping voice, go up the scale and down the scale, say it as an elephant would say it – use lots of imagination!

You also need to help children develop their own strategies for mental calculations. There are no 'proper' methods – children can choose whatever method suits them best. You need to point this out and draw attention to the different ways of doing things, by asking children as often as possible how they worked things out.

For example, to work out $8 + 7$, you could make the 8 up to 10 by adding 2, and then add the extra 5. You might double 8 and subtract 1, or double 7 and add 1. You could think of it as $4 + 4 + 4 + 3$. You could even start with 20, then take away 2, and then 3.

Responding to children's answers

Praise is important, so how do you avoid discouragement when children give 'wrong' answers? Rather than saying 'yes' or 'no' to right or wrong answers, you can try saying:

- Has anyone got a different answer?
- What do other people think?
- Are there any other possibilities?
- How did you work that out? Did anyone do it a different way?
- How could we check that?

It is easier for children to come up with acceptable answers if occasionally you build in a longer thinking time for those who find it difficult. You could also ask children to agree an answer with a partner before going 'public'. More open-ended questions allow a wider range of possible answers and help to encourage the more diffident. For example:

- Which pairs of numbers have a difference of 2?

- The answer is 3. What was the question?

- How could you pay for a lollipop costing 8p?

- What numbers can you make with the digits 1, 2 and 3?

- Can you estimate the height of this room, or how much this jug holds, or the number of words in this rhyme…?

- I know that $2 + 5$ is 7, so what else do I know?

  For example,

$5 + 2 = 7$	$7 - 5 = 2$	$7 - 2 = 5$	
$3 + 5 = 8$	$2 + 6 = 8$	$1 + 5 = 6$	$2 + 4 = 6$
$12 + 5 = 17$	$2 + 15 = 17$	$20 + 50 = 70$	

The importance of counting

Almost any session can start with a quick counting activity. It's certainly worth checking when children start school, and then at the start of each term, which children are confident with early counting activities.

Level 1

- Choose a number. Show me using your fingers. Write it in the air.
- Say *1, 2, 3*... very slowly, very loudly, backwards, clapping as you say it...
- Whose birthday is it today? Let's clap how old you are.
- Let's say or sing together: *One, two – three, four, five. Once I caught a fish alive...*, or: *Ten green bottles...*, or: *One, two, three, four. Mary at the cottage door...*
- Count these cubes. They are all the same size and shape.
  Now count these bricks. They are different sizes and shapes.
- These counters are arranged in a line. Can you count them?
  Count these (arranged randomly). You can move them as you count.
  Now count these. You can touch them if you want to, but don't move them.
  Now count these – but without touching them. How many are there?
- Count these spots – stuck on A4 cards – arranged in a straight line, in a regular pattern, arranged randomly.
- Count this tower of jumbo bricks. Now lay them in a long line on the floor.
  How many jumbo bricks now?
- Count the children in the group. There is one chair for each child.
  How many chairs are there?
- Count in your head till I say stop. What number did you reach?
  Now count aloud for me to that number.
- How many fingers am I holding up? Count them to yourself and then tell me.
- Count these cubes into this box. I've taken out three. How many are still in the box?
- I'll say a number, and you count on – or back – from there.
- What number comes after 3? What number comes before 5? Two before 4?
- Count some things you can't touch or reach: the window panes, the chairs in the room, the birds in the picture on the wall, the dogs on the 'pets' graph ...
- If we counted round the circle starting with Mary with 5, who would say 11?
  Think in your heads and tell me who it would be.
- Count these chime bar sounds to yourself, then tell me how many you heard – first at regular intervals, then irregular.
- Look at these cards with spots on (no more than 10, in identifiable groups such as twos and threes). Can you say how many spots there are without counting one by one?
  How did you know?
- Point to the fourth counter in this row. What colour is the seventh counter?
  Which counter is one before the blue one? Point to the third red counter.

Level 2

- Make a number strip 20 squares long. Write the numbers on it.
- Say: *One two, buckle my shoe…*
  or: *Two, four, six, eight. Mary at the garden gate…*
- Count the spots on these domino doubles.
  How many altogether is double six, double three, double five…?
- Count the even numbers. Count the odd numbers. Now count them backwards.
- Let's count all our shoes in turn. Whisper your right shoe number. Shout your left shoe number. Which numbers did we whisper? Which did we shout?
- Count in twos, starting with 6. Will we get to 17? How do you know?
- Take 12 counters. Count them onto the table one at a time, two at a time, three at a time, four at a time.
- What number is the third before 9? The fourth after 6?
- Look at these dominoes as I hold them up. Put up your hand if you see one with 7 spots on.
- Look at these cards with spots on (no more than 10, randomly arranged, but in identifiable groups such as twos, threes or fours). Can you say how many spots there are without counting one by one? How did you know?
- Estimate how many spots there are on these cards when I hold them up briefly. Who thinks there are more than 12? Can you explain why?
- Count in tens to 100, and then back to nought.
- Now start at 5 and count in tens. Will you say 43? How do you know?
- Count backwards in ones from 0.

Level 3

- Take 30 counters. Count them one at a time, two at a time, three at a time.
- How many children in the group? How many legs, arms, eyes, fingers, toes…?
- What number is the third before 21? What number is the fourth after 18?
- Count in threes to 30. Count in fours to 24.
- Start at 2 and count in threes. Start at 5 and count in fours.
- Start at 30 and count backwards in threes. Now start at 31.
- Start at 40 and count backwards in fours. Now start at 42.
- Count in twenties to 200. Now count backwards in twenties to zero.
- Count in hundreds to 1000 and back again.
- Count backwards in tens from 0.
- If everyone wore a cardigan with 5 buttons, how many buttons would there be altogether? How did you work it out?
- How many words do you think there are on this page of your reading book? What is a good way to estimate?

Rhymes

Saying rhymes in unison with other children can generate confidence in those who are reluctant to speak. The rhythm in a simple rhyme often helps children to remember counting sequences. Other rhymes can provide a context for simple calculations.

My money-box is round and blue.
Its hole is very wide.
I'm going to save ten pennies
And drop them down inside.

One, two, three...

Vary the number of pennies saved.

Ten fat sausages sizzling in the pan.
One went POP and one went BANG!

Eight fat sausages...

Go on from here.
Try starting with nine sausages.

One candle on my birthday cake
Is burning very bright.
I'm lighting one more candle,
And two are now alight.

Two candles on my birthday cake...

Go on from here.
Also try lighting two more candles each time.
Try starting with a bigger number and changing the third line to: 'I'm blowing out one candle'.

Here comes the bus. It's going to stop.
Two go inside and three on top.

How many people got on the bus?

Vary the numbers going inside and on top.

Seven big bananas are growing on the tree.
Katy shook it hard – and down came three!

How many bananas were left?

Vary the number of bananas on the tree and the child's name.

Dad put some cakes on a big square plate.
Kim ate three – and then there were eight.

How many cakes did Dad put on the plate?

Vary the number of cakes eaten and the name.

Plant three daffodils
In a straight line.
How many more must I plant
In order to make nine?

Vary the number of daffodils planted.

Two red robins had six crusts of bread.
How many of the crusts was each robin fed?

Vary the numbers of robins and crusts.

You will find more examples of rhymes and counting activities in *Talking Points*, by Anita Straker, published by Cambridge University Press (ISBN 0 521 44758 5).

Assessing children's achievements

Most of your assessment of what children are achieving in their mental mathematics will be informal, done by watching and listening to them carefully. Judgements about their use of vocabulary, their accuracy and speed of recall of mathematical facts, and whether they can manage without using their fingers, are easier to make. It is more difficult to judge their 'at homeness' with number, their use of imagery and their confidence with different methods and strategies. A few questions you could keep in mind are these.

- Are children 'at home' with numbers? Can they:
  - make a good estimate of a number in a group;
  - recognise which number operation is needed to solve a problem;
  - recall quickly number facts such as number bonds, odds and evens, doubles and halves, multiplication tables, simple squares or square roots such as $9 = 3 \times 3$, relationships between measures;
  - carry out more than one single step operation;
  - choose suitable units and make sensible estimates of measurements?

- Do they use what they already know to derive an answer: for example, place value or close relationships to other numbers or to other calculations? For example,
  6 + 7 is 13 because it's two sixes plus 1, or two sevens take away 1.
  9 + 9 must be 18 because it's the same as 10 + 10 take away 2.
  20 + 40 = 60 because 2 + 4 = 6.
  4 × 6 must be 24 because 4 × 3 is 12.

- Do they know when their answers are right? For example,
  - are they aware of an approximate or 'rough' value for a calculation:
    I think 9 and 19 must be about 30, because 10 and 20 is 30;
  - are they aware of the size of the answer, or the range that it must lie in:
    half of 13 must be between 10 and 5, because half of 20 is 10 and half of 10 is 5;
  - do they know whether their answer should be: *be odd or even, end in zero, have two digits, be whole or fractional, positive or negative …;*
  - do they make sensible decisions about rounding up or down:
    13 ÷ 6 is 2 and a bit, but if one box holds 6 eggs I would need 3 boxes for 13 eggs;
  - can they check a result by doing it different way:
    9 take away 6 must be 3 because 3 plus 6 is 9.
    15 × 3 is 45, because 3 lots of 10 plus 3 lots of 5 is 45, and also because 15 + 15 is 30, and 15 more is 45?

- Are they adopting flexible methods of working, and can they explain their methods and their reasoning? For example,
  I worked out 17 − 9 in two steps. First 17 − 7, which is 10, and then 10 − 2, which is 8.
  I added 13 and 15 together. I did the tens first and got 20, and then I did the units and I got 8, so altogether it's 28.

Part 2: Oral work

These activities are intended to be led by you or by a classroom assistant. Some are suitable for a whole class and others for small groups. Most will take from five to ten minutes but some may need a little longer. In many of the activities no writing is needed, though children could record their answers in the ways described on page 3; in others, it is helpful to tabulate some of the results in order to look for patterns.

On the spot

Objectives
Level 1:
understanding of small numbers.

Organisation
Work with a group of up to four children.

Words to stress
one, two, three, ...

What you need
You need 10 sheets of paper, about A4 size, and about 50 small objects such as cubes, beans or bottle tops. Draw four large spots on each sheet of paper, varying their spacing.

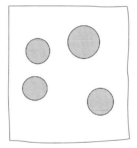 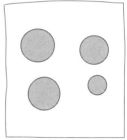

What to do
Set out the sheets of paper with the spotty side upwards. Ask different children to count out four cubes onto each sheet, placing them on the spots, while saying one, two, three, four.

Now put the cubes to one side and turn the sheets over. Ask the children to imagine putting four cubes on each blank sheet. Taking turns, can they point on each sheet to where their four cubes will go? Afterwards, count out the cubes. Spend some time arranging them in patterns of 2 and 2, 1 and 3, close together, far apart, in a line, ..., and recounting them.

Now ask the children to close their eyes and imagine four cubes. Then ask:

- What colour are your cubes? Are they all the same?
- Imagine taking away one cube. How many are left?
- Imagine putting the cube back. How many cubes now?

Caterpillars

Objectives
Level 1:
ordering numbers to 10.

Organisation
Work with a group of about four children. Once they know the game, they can carry on by themselves for a while.

Words to stress
one, two, three, ...;
order, first, second, ...;
before, after, next.

What you need
You need a set of cards numbered from 1 to 10 for each child. Provide everyone with a starter card of a caterpillar face, or get them to design and make their own.

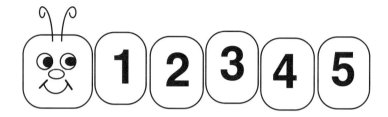

What to do
Shuffle the sets of numbered cards together. Spread them out face down. Ask the children to take turns to pick up a card. The aim is to make a caterpillar by collecting all the cards from 1 to 10 and placing them in order. If the number has already been collected it is replaced face down. Ask:

- What number is that? Where will you put it?
- Which number will go in third place?
- What number will go before/after 5?
- What will be between 4 and 6?

 Patterns

Objectives
Level 1:
repeating patterns.

Organisation
Work with a group of any size. Children can continue the activity on their own in pairs.

Words to stress
one, two, three, ...;
order, first, second, ...;
before, after, next.

What you need
You need bricks, beads, buttons or counters in different colours and shapes, some coins and a piece of A4 paper.

What to do
Ask the children to close their eyes. Set out in a line a repeated pattern using a selection of the materials. Cover part of the pattern with the piece of paper. Ask the children to open their eyes and to work out which coins or bricks, and how many, are hidden.

What's missing?

Objectives
Level 1:
ordering numbers to 10.

Organisation
Work with a group of three or four children. Children can continue the games by themseleves.

Words to stress
before, after, next; one more, one less.

What you need
You need a set of cards either numbered from 1 to 10, or with dot patterns from 1 to 10. You also need a selection of small objects: dice, buttons, beans, …

What to do
Game 1
Put the cards face down and shuffle them. Take one without looking at it and hide it. Then turn the rest face up. The children have to identify which card is missing.

Game 2
Set out all the numbered cards face up. Put different objects by each: four beans next to the numeral 4, and so on. While the children close their eyes, remove one of the objects from one of the groups. They must then work out what has gone.

 Feely bag

Objectives
Level 1:
identification of shapes.

Organisation
Work with a group of up to eight children.

Words to stress
round, square, triangular, circular; hard, soft, thick, thin, long, short, rough, smooth, straight, curved.

What you need
You need a draw-string bag and pairs of objects: for example, two balls, oranges, identical beads, cubes, cuboid bricks, cones, pencils, coins, …

What to do
Put one of each object in the bag and pull the string tight. Pass the bag round the group, asking each child in turn to feel an object and point out its partner on the table. Ask:

- How can you tell its the orange?
  How do you know it's not the ball?
- Can you describe the object you are feeling to us?
- How many flat sides/straight edges can you feel?
- Which shape was the easiest to identify? Why?

Remove the objects in the centre and repeat the activity.

6 Give-away

Objectives
Level 1:
counting to 10 and beyond.

Organisation
Work with a group of up to four children. Children can continue the game on their own.

Words to stress
one, two, three, ...; right, left.

What you need
You need a dice, and ten counters (or buttons or shells) counted out for each child.

What to do
Children should take turns to throw the dice. They give that number of counters to the child on their right (or all their counters if they do not have enough). The dice is then passed to the left.

The winner can be the first to get rid of all their counters, or the one with the most counters after three rounds. An extra rule could be that the counters to be given away must all be different colours as far as possible, or all the same colour. Ask the children:

- How many counters do you have now? Can you count them? Can you count them without touching them?
- When Dan has given you his three counters, how many will you have then? How many will Dan have left?

7 Longer and shorter

Objectives
Level 1:
counting;
comparison of lengths.

Organisation
Work with a small group. Up to six children is best.

Words to stress
one, two, three, ...;
longer, shorter;
more, fewer, difference.

What you need
Prepare some sheets of paper on which lines of various lengths have been drawn: straight, curved or a mixture. You also need several wooden cubes, cotton reels, beans, 2p coins, or anything that can be used as units of measure.

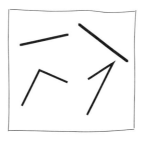

[NOTE: Alternatively, you could draw shapes with straight/curved edges for children to investigate areas to be covered.]

What to do

Ask the children to find which line is the longest. Ask them:

- On which line do you think you could fit the most cubes? Now check. How many cubes have you put along it?
- Can you estimate how many cubes will fit on this line?
- Is this line longer or shorter than this one? How much longer/shorter? What is the difference?
- Can you draw a straight line which will hold just five cubes? Now try a curved line.
- Is there any way in which you can fit more beans on the line? (*For example, beans could go across the line, rather than end to end, or cotton reels could stand on a circular face.*)
- If you put 2p coins along this line rather than wooden cubes, would you need more or fewer?

Straw people

Objectives

Level 1:
counting to 10;
simple sums and differences.

Organisation

Work with a group of up to eight children.

Words to stress

one, two, three, …;
more, fewer;
how many altogether;
longer, taller, shorter.

What you need

You need some circles of card for heads, and plenty of drinking straws cut into 5 centimetre lengths.

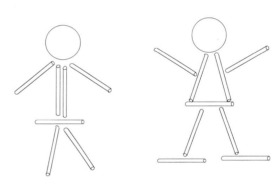

What to do

Ask the children to make a person using the straws and then to give their person a name. Then ask them:

- How many straws did you use? How did you count?
- Who used the same number of straws as Amin?
- Did you use more/fewer straws than Kelly? How many more/fewer?
- How many arms on these three people? How many legs?
- Whose person is tallest/shortest?
- How could you make your person taller?
- If you took away this straw, how many would be left?
- If you used two more straws to make longer arms, how many straws would you have used then?
- How many straws altogether for these two people?

9 Card games

Objectives
Level 1:
addition and subtraction facts to 6.

Organisation
Work with a group of three or four children. After a while, children can continue the games on their own.

Words to stress
add, sum, total, more, less, subtract, difference, multiply, product.

What you need
Make four sets of cards numbered from 0 to 3.

What to do
Game 1
Shuffle the cards. Divide them into two packs and place these face down. Children take turns to take a card from each pack and add the two numbers. During play, use questions like these, varying the vocabulary.

- What is the sum of your two numbers? What do they total? Is that more or less than 5?
- What is the difference between 5 and your total?

As a variation, find the difference between the two numbers. More advanced groups could find the product.

Game 2
Shuffle the cards and spread them out face down. Children take turns to turn over a pair of cards. If the total is 3, they keep the pair. Otherwise the two cards are replaced face down. The child with the most pairs at the end of the game is the winner.

Game 3
Shuffle the cards and put them face down in a single pile. Children take turns to take a card from the top of the pack. They must then say what they would add to the number drawn to make 5. If they are correct, they keep the card. Otherwise it is returned to the bottom of the pile. Ask:

- What must you add to ... to make 5?
- How could you check that?

10 Boxes

Objectives
Level 1:
counting to 10 and beyond;
relative size;
simple comparisons of capacity.

Organisation
Work with a small group of up to eight children.

Words to stress
one, two, three, ...;
full, empty;
inside, outside;
big, small.

What you need
You need boxes and tins of different sizes and shapes, with different kinds of lids. Put some sand, marbles, pebbles, rice, screwed up bits of paper, ... inside some of them.

What to do
Set out the containers so that everyone can see them. Ask:

- Which is the tallest container? Which is the shortest? Can you arrange them in order of their heights?
- Which is the fattest/thinnest/widest/most narrow?
- What shape is this lid? And this one? Which is the biggest round lid?
- How many of the containers have flat lids?
- Look at the containers. How many do you think you could you stack up, one on top of the other? How tall would the stack be? Can you show me with your hands?
- What do you imagine could be inside this box (rattle it)? Could it be sand, marbles, a ball, ...? What couldn't it be?
- Without peeping, put you hand inside and feel what is in there. Don't tell us but describe it so that we can guess.
- Imagine a banana. Would it fit inside this tin? What about a tennis ball?
- Tell me some things that you think would fit in this box. What wouldn't fit in it?
- Do you think this container would fit inside this one? Is there another one that would fit inside both of them?
- How many cotton reels do you think you could pack into this box? Guess first and then we'll try. Could we pack more cotton reels in if we organised them differently?

11 Straws

Objectives
Levels 1, 2:
counting to 20 or beyond;
measuring lengths.

Organisation
Work with a group of up to eight children.

Words to stress
one, two, three, …;
distance, length;
longer, shorter,
further, closer;
more, fewer, difference.

What you need
You need five drinking straws cut in half to make 10 short straws, and some other things that can be used as measures of length: for example, pencils, rods, paper clips. Each child will need a different coloured counter to use as a marker.

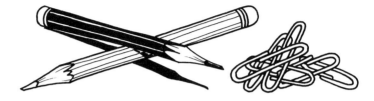

What to do
Tell the children to imagine the 10 straws laid end to end on the table. Ask them to estimate how far the straws will reach and, one by one, to put their counter down to mark the point. Then lay out the straws. Ask the children:

- Whose estimate is closest? Whose is the furthest away? How many straws between them?
- This position marks a length of 10 straws. Can you move your marker to where you think 15 straws would reach.
- If we measured the width of the door with straws, how many do you imagine it would be?
- Can you tell me any things that are about the same length as one straw? Five straws? Ten?

Repeat the activity and type of questions with other units.

12 Magic wand

Objectives
Levels 1, 2:
counting on.

Organisation
Work with six children.

Words to stress
how many more?
add, plus, difference.

What you need
You need eight cubes linked to make a 'wand'.

What to do
Show the children the wand and count the cubes to confirm that the 'magic number' is 8. Hide the wand behind your back, and break it into two pieces. Keep one piece hidden. Show the children the other and count the cubes. Ask them:

- How many more to make eight?
- What must we add to … to make 8?

Repeat several times, then try a wand of a different length.

13) Wriggly worms

Objectives

Levels 1, 2:
counting to 20 or beyond;
repeating patterns.

Organisation

Work with a group of
four or five children.

Words to stress

add, sum, total,
altogether;
more, fewer.

What you need

You need a dice, plenty of large coloured counters, some
circles of plain card and a selection of coloured pens.

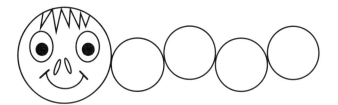

What to do

Each child should make a face for their worm and place it on
the table. They then take turns to roll the dice and add that
number of counters to their worm's body. The winner is the
child with the most counters at the end of a given number of
turns, or who first makes a worm of a given length.

According their attainment, you can ask each child to:

- make a worm in one colour;
- add different colours on each turn, thus recording the
  number thrown;
- build a pattern such as *red, blue, red, blue, ...* or *green, green,
  yellow, green, green, yellow, ...*

During play you can ask questions like:

- What number did you roll? Is that more or less than 3?
- How many counters in your worm now?
- Who has a total of 11 counters?
- Can you point to the seventh counter in your worm?
- How many would you have if you had one more, one
  fewer, two more, two fewer, ... counters?
- How many counters will you have altogether if you count
  on 3 from 6?
- Who has the longest/shortest worm?
- How much longer/shorter is that worm than this one?
- In the middle of your worm there are two pink then five
  black counters? How many is that altogether?
- Can you point to the fifth red counter? What position is
  that in your worm?
- If you continued your worm pattern of two red, three
  green, would the 17th counter be red or green?

14 Capitals

Objectives

Levels 1, 2:
counting to 10;
recognition of straight
and curved lines.

Organisation

Work with a group of
any size, or the whole
class.

Words to stress

how many?
more, fewer;
curved, straight;
up, down, left, right.

What you need

You need a board or large sheet of paper on which to draw
letters or to keep a record.

What to do

Ask the children to imagine a capital letter **A**. Then ask them
to draw it in the air in front of them. Ask them to describe
how they are drawing the lines: for example, down to the
left, down to the right, across from left to right. Then ask:

- Did you draw curved or straight lines?
- How many straight lines did you draw? *(3)*

Then ask them to imagine a letter **D** and repeat the questions.
Try some more letters, such as **C**, **Z** or **R**. Then ask:

- Can you think of some capital letters that are made from
  only straight lines? *(A, E, F, H, I, K, L, M, N, T, V, W, X, Y,
  Z. There is no need to find them all at this stage.)*
- Are any letters made from just one straight line? *(One: I)*
- Is there a letter made from just 2 straight lines? Can you
  draw it in the air for me? How many of these letters are
  there altogether? *(Four: L, T, V, X)*
- Who can think of a letter made from just 3 straight lines?
  Are there any more? How many of these letters are there
  altogether? *(Seven: A, F, H, K, N, Y, Z)*
- Which letters are made from 4 straight lines? *(E, M, W)*

You could record the data in a table.

Number of lines in the letter	Number of letters
One line	1
Two lines	4
Three lines	7
Four lines	3

Then ask questions about the data.

- Are there more letters with 3 straight lines or more with 2 straight lines? How many more/fewer?
  (Three more with 3 lines that with 2 lines)
- How many letters with 4 lines are there? *(3)*
- For which sort of letter is there only one? *(1 line)*

---

15 Lollipop

Objectives
Levels 1, 2:
addition of coins to 6p.

Organisation
Work with a group of any size, or the whole class.

Words to stress
how much?
sum, plus, total, value.

What you need
You need a board or large sheet of paper on which to keep a record.

What to do
Tell the children to imagine that they are buying a lollipop. They have only 1p and 2p coins to pay with. They might like some coins to experiment with at first, but encourage them to use their imaginations and to calculate mentally as much as possible. Ask them:

- How could you pay for a lollipop costing 3p? Which coins would you use?
- Does the order of the coins matter? Does 2p + 1p have the same value as 1p + 2p?
- How many different ways can you make a total of 3p? *(Two ways: one 2p and one 1p, or three 1p)*
- What if the lollipop cost 4p? How many different ways of paying for it are there now? *(Three ways: two 2p, or one 2p and two 1p, or four 1p)*
- What if the lollipop cost 5p? *(Three ways: two 2p and one 1p, or one 2p and three 1p, or five 1p)*
- What about lollipops costing 1p or 2p? *(1 and 2 different ways respectively)*
- Could we record all our findings in a table?
- Can you predict how many different ways there are to pay for a lollipop costing 6p? *(4)*

16   I spy

Objectives
Levels 1, 2:
properties of shapes.

Organisation
Work with a group of up to 8 children.

Words to stress
names of shapes;
side, corner;
edge, face, corner.

What you need
You need a set of assorted shapes: 3D or 2D.

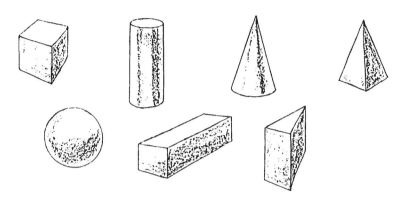

What to do
Put the shapes where all the children can see them and play *I spy…* Say things like: I spy with my little eye, a shape…

- beginning with C (cube, cuboid, circle, cylinder);
- with six sides (hexagon);
- with four corners (square, rectangle, tetrahedron);
- that will roll (sphere, cylinder, cone);
- with a point at the top (cone or pyramid);
- with five faces (triangular prism, square pyramid).

After a while, put the shapes away and tell the children they are to imagine the shapes while the game continues.

17   Kangaroo

Objectives
Level 2:
odd and even numbers.

Organisation
Work with a group of four or five children.

Words to stress
odd, even, equal.

What you need
You need a 0 to 20 number line, a felt pen or other means of marking spaces on the number line, and a counter (kangaroo).

What to do
Put the counter on the number line at 0. Show the children how the 'kangaroo' can make two equal jumps along the line to land on a number. Then ask them to imagine where the kangaroo would land if it made two equal jumps of 3 (or any other number). The jumps can be checked using the kangaroo if necessary. Each time mark the number reached, perhaps by ringing it with a felt pen. Ask:

- Where would you land with two equal jumps of 6?
- Can you land on 10 in two equal jumps? On 18?
- Can you land on 9 in two equal jumps? What about 15?
- What do you notice about all the numbers we have marked? Are there any others that you think we should mark?
- Are there any numbers you will never land on? Why not?
- What about numbers beyond the number line. Could you land on 24 in two equal jumps? Or 25?
- What if we started at 3 instead of 0? Or 2?
- What if we made three equal jumps?

 ## Shapes from squares

Objectives
Level 2:
properties of shapes;
symmetry.

Organisation
Work with a group of any size, or the whole class.

Words to stress
square;
flip, turn, reflect.

What you need
You need some gummed paper squares and squared paper to stick them on, or some square tiles.

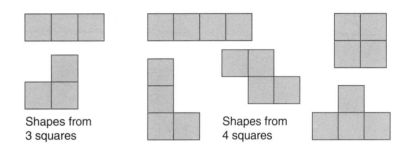

Shapes from 3 squares

Shapes from 4 squares

What to do
Ask the children to make a pattern with three squares. Discuss with them before they begin how they imagine it will look. Then ask them to make it. At first children are likely to arrange the squares randomly, to overlap them or to leave gaps. At this stage ask:

- Is that how you imagined your pattern would be?
- What colours have you used? Who else has used them?
- Are there any patterns/shapes that are similar?
- Which colour is on the left of your pattern? At the top?
- If we turned that pattern, would it look like this one?

Introduce the idea that each square must touch at least one other without overlaps, and explore the patterns and shapes further. Refine this idea to looking for those shapes in which the squares touch each other tidily along an edge. Compare shapes that are the 'same' when reflected or rotated, so that the children conclude that only two shapes are possible.

The activity can be extended later to four squares.

Splodges

Objectives

Level 2:
counting to 10 and
beyond;
one/two more or less;
simple comparisons of
areas;
simple graphs.

Organisation

Work with a group of six
to eight children.

Words to stress

how many?
more, fewer, most, least.

What you need

You need a sheet of A1 paper, a pencil and a felt pen, and
plenty of large counters in different colours. Use the pencil
to draw several squares on the paper, each about 3 inches by
3 inches, but varying in size with some a little larger and
some a little smaller. Space the squares well apart.

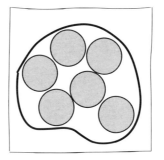

What to do

Use the felt pen to draw a puddle shape inside one of the
squares. Tell the children that this is a splodge. Ask one of
the children to guess first and then find out how many red
counters will fit inside the splodge. Then ask:

- How many counters has Ella fitted in?
- Could we fit in more counters if we rearranged them?

Invite other children to try and squeeze in more counters
until everyone is convinced that the maximum has been
found. Then ask one of the children to record the number at
the side of the splodge. Repeat with the other squares, using
counters of a different colour each time. Then ask, where
necessary checking by counting:

- Which splodge has the most/least counters?
- Which splodge has one more counter than this one?
- Which has two fewer than this one?
- Which splodge has the biggest area? How do you know?
- Could you draw a splodge which would hold just four
  counters? Just 10 counters?

Take one of the sets of counters and ask a child to say how
many there are. Then ask that child to rearrange the counters
in a straight line. Ask another child to say how many
counters there are in the line. (*Those with a full understanding
of the conservation of number will not need to recount.*)

Repeat with the other sets of counters until they are lined up with a common base line.

Our splodges

The difference between the biggest splodge and the smallest splodge was five counters.

Ask questions like:

- What colour is the line with 5 counters?
- How many counters in the red line?
- Which line has two more counters than the blue one?

---

(20) Estimating beans

Objectives
Level 2:
estimates and counting to 10 and beyond;
simple differences in the range 1 to 20.

Organisation
Work with a group of up to eight children.

Words to stress
how many?
estimate, guess, about;
more, less, most, least;
difference.

What you need
You need some small see-through jars with lids. Put from 5 to 15 large dried beans, wooden beads or small pebbles in each jar. You also need a 1 to 20 number line, and a differently coloured counter for each child, plus a black one for yourself.

| 1 | 2 | 3 | 4 | ... | 17 | 18 | 19 | 20 |

What to do
Take a jar and pass it round the group. Let each child guess how many beans there are in the jar and record their estimate by placing their counter on the number line. Open the jar and let one child count the beans and record that number with the black counter. Then ask:

- Was Sam's estimate more or less than Jade's?
- Whose estimate was the least? Whose was the most?
- Whose estimate was closest to the real number? How close was it? Whose was furthest away? How far was it?
- How many more did Winston guess than Ali? What was the difference between their two guesses? Was Winston or Ali closer to the real number?

Repeat with other jars with different contents.

Musical numbers

Objectives
Level 2:
properties of numbers:
odd and even numbers,
doubles and halves.

Organisation
Work in the hall with a
group of any size, or a
whole class.

Words to stress
double, half;
odd, even;
more, less.

What you need
You need a number line to walk on, either chalked on the floor, made from hoops, or from a roll of wallpaper. Number the spaces from 1 to 10 (or 20). You also need a tape recorder and music.

What to do
Ten children should stand on the number line facing towards 10. The rest complete a circle from 10 back to 1. The children should move round the circle as you play some music and should stop when the music stops. They are 'out' according to the rule you call: for example, numbers less than 4, odd numbers, even numbers, half of 8, double 3, numbers that divide exactly by 5, numbers which are 2 steps from 7.

 What's the question?

Objectives
Level 2:
addition and
subtraction.

Organisation
Work with a group of
any size, or the whole
class.

Words to stress
add, plus, sum, total;
more, less;
count on, count back;
take away, minus,
subtract, difference.

What you need
A board or wallchart on which to keep a record.

What to do
Choose any two numbers: for example, 2 and 5. Ask the children to make up different questions using the numbers. Encourage them to think of:

- What is 2 add 5?
- 2 plus 5 equals ...?
- What is the sum of (or total of) 2 and 5?
- If you count on 5 from 2 you get to ...?
- What is 5 more than 2?
- What should we add to 2 to make 5?
- What is 5 take away 2?
- 5 minus 2 equals ...?
- If we subtract 2 from 5, we get ...? What about 5 from 2?
- What is the difference between 5 and 2?
- If you count back 2 from 5 you get to ...?
- How many more than 2 is 5?
- When I take 5 from a number I get 2. What is the number?
- I added 2 and got 5? What did I start with?

23 Peek-a-boo

Objectives
Level 2:
names and properties
of 2D shapes.

Organisation
Work with about four
to six children.

Words to stress
names of shapes;
pointed, curved, sloping,
rounded, straight;
edge, corner;
end, top, bottom.

If appropriate:
right angle.

What you need
You need a box of assorted flat shapes and a large thin book
to make a screen between you and the children.

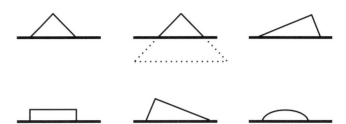

What to do
Choose a shape without letting the children see it, and show
a tiny part of it above the screen, perhaps a corner or an edge.
Ask children to take turns to guess what the shape might be.
Each time anyone makes a guess, they must say why they
think it might be such a shape. They are then told yes or no.
After each guess, take the shape down behind the screen and
turn it so that a different part is shown. Ask them:

• What might the shape be? Why do you think so?
• Could it be any other shape ? Why?

---

24 Shapes from cubes

Objectives
Level 2:
relative positions.

Organisation
Work with about six
children.

Words to stress
long, short;
edge, corner;
end, top, bottom, left,
right, above, below, over,
under, beside, next to.

What you need
Multilink cubes and a large thin book to make a screen.

What to do
Make a shape from three or four cubes, keeping it hidden.
Tell the children how you are making your shape, cube by
cube, so that they can make one the same as yours. For
example: *Take a green cube. Put a second green cube on top of
it. Put a pink cube to the right of the top green cube. Put a red cube
behind the pink cube.* Then ask the children:

• Is your shape the same as mine?
• On your shape, which cube is in front of the red one?
• If I turn my shape like this, where is the pink cube now?

25 What's in the bag?

Objectives
Level 2:
number patterns;
likelihood.

Organisation
Work with a small group.

Words to stress
how many?
likely, probably;
cube;
more, less.

What you need
You need a small draw-string bag. Put six cubes in it: four red and two blue.

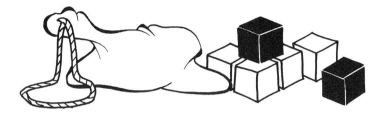

What to do
Pass the bag around the group for the children to feel the contents without opening the bag. Ask the children to keep their thoughts to themselves until each child has had a turn. Then ask:

- What do you imagine is in the bag? What shape are they? How many of them are there?
- Imagine a cube. How many corners does it have? *(8)* How many faces? *(6)*

Pass the bag around again. This time each child should take out just one cube, hold it up to show the other children, then put it back. Allow several draws. Get each child to make conjectures about the contents of the bag after each draw.

- What colour is that cube? What colour do you think the rest of the cubes are?
- How many red cubes do you think there are? How many blue cubes?
- Do you think that there is a yellow cube in the bag?

(Children may jump to conclusions. For example, if the first cube drawn out is red, they may think that all the cubes are red. Try to get them to modify what they think as they acquire more information. Eventually they should conclude that the cubes are of two colours, some red and some blue, with probably more red than blue.)

26 Paper plates

Objectives
Level 2:
simple division.

What you need
You need about 10 paper plates and 20 cubes (or walnuts, beans, shells, small dolls, farm animals, or any other small objects that will interest the children).

Organisation
Work with a group of up to six children.

Words to stress
enough;
share, divide.

What to do
Put out five plates and 15 cubes. Practise counting out the cubes in twos, threes and fives. Try sharing them among the plates one at a time. Then ask:

- Do you think that there are enough cubes to put two on each plate? *(Yes)* Three on each plate? *(Yes)*
- Are there enough to put four on each plate? *(No)*
- On how many plates could you put five cubes? *(3)*
- If a plate will hold only 10 cubes, how many plates will I need for all 15 of these cubes? *(2)*

Only after the children have thought mentally about the problem should the cubes be counted onto the plates.

27 Potatoes

Objectives
Level 2:
comparison of lengths and weights.

Organisation
Work with a group of about six children.

Words to stress
longest, shortest;
height, width;
largest, smallest;
heaviest, lightest.

What you need
You need a large, clean potato and a piece of string for each child, and a pair of scissors between three. You also need a beam balance.

What to do
Group the children in threes. Ask each group to guess which of their potatoes is the heaviest. Then ask:

- How could you check? *(For example, compare potatoes in pairs, one in each hand, or on the beam balance. Each time, eliminate the lighter of the two potatoes.)*
- Do you think the heaviest potato is the fattest?
  How could you check? *(For example, stand the potatoes side by side and compare heights or widths. Another way is to use a string to measure round a potato in various places until its largest girth is found. The string can then be cut to length. After each potato has been measured, the lengths of all the strings can be compared to find out which potato is the fattest.)*

(28) Picnic

Objectives
Level 2:
simple fractions.

Organisation
Work with a group of up to eight children.

Words to stress
half, quarter;
names of shapes.

What you need
Nothing.

What to do
Ask the children to imagine what they are going to take to eat on a picnic. Then ask:

- Suppose we took a big round pizza. What shape is that? *(Circular)* Can you draw it in the air?
- What if you wanted to share the pizza with a friend? How many pieces would you cut it into? *(2)*
  What would each piece look like? *(A semi-circle)*
- Suppose we had a sandwich. What shape is that? *(Let's call it a square.)*
- If you cut the sandwich in half, what would each half look like? Can you draw one half?
  Did everyone draw the same shape? *(Probably not. One half could be a rectangle, or a triangle, or any other shape made by cutting through the centre of the square with a straight line.)*
- What if we took some samosas? What do they look like? Can you draw one in the air?
- If we cut a triangular samosa in half, how many people could have a piece? *(2)*
  What shape would one half be? *(Triangular)*
- Suppose you had six chocolate muffins on your picnic, and you gave half of them to Abu. How many would he get? *(3)* What if you had three muffins? *(One and a half)*
- If four people wanted to share the big round pizza, what fraction would you each get? *(One quarter)*
  Can you draw its shape in the air?

- There are eight cans of fizzy drink for the picnic. How many cans each would the four people get? *(2)*
- If you drank one quarter of a bottle of lemonade, how much would be left? *(Three quarters)*
- If four people each drank half a litre of orangeade, how much did they drink altogether? *(2 litres)*

 ## Lines and blobs

Objectives
Levels 2, 3:
number patterns;
odd and even numbers.

Organisation
Work with a group of any size, or the whole class.

Words to stress
difference;
odd, even.

What you need
You need a board or wallchart on which to draw and on which to keep a record.

What to do
Show the children the first part of this pattern and ask them to describe it. They should see that there are three blobs, one at the top and two at the bottom, joined by two lines.

Tell them that this is the start of a pattern and ask them how they think it will continue. They will have various suggestions but tell them that today you are going to draw the next part of the pattern as shown in the diagram above. Then ask:

- How many lines in the second part? *(4)* Blobs? *(5)*
  How many more blobs than lines? *(1)*
- What will the next part of the pattern look like?
  How many lines? *(6)* How many blobs? *(7)*
  How many more blobs than lines? *(1)*
- How will the pattern continue?
  How many lines? *(Two more than the one before)*
  How many blobs? *(Two more than the one before, and always one more than the number of lines)*
- Do you recognise the pattern made by the blobs? *(Even numbers)* The lines? *(Odd numbers)*
- How many blobs in the fifth part of the pattern? *(10)*
  In the 20th part? *(40)*

30 Dozens

Objectives
Level 3:
number bonds to 20.

Organisation
Work with a group of
any size, or a whole
class.

Words to stress
add, subtract,
sum, total, difference.

What you need
For a small group you need a set of cards numbered from 1
to 20. For a large group working in pairs, you could draw
and then photocopy a 5×4 grid of numbers from 1 to 20 for
each pair to cut out and use as cards.

What to do
First ask the children to choose pairs of cards that total 12 and
to place them side by side. Ask them:

• How many of the cards can you use? *(Maximum is 10)*

Now ask the children to start again, but this time each pair
may have either a sum or a difference of 12.

• How many of the cards can you use? *(Maximum is 16)*
• What if you can group together any number of cards?
  *(You can use them all: for example: $20 - 8$, $19 - 13 + 6$,
  $18 - 15 + 9$, $17 - 7 + 2$, $16 - 10 - 3 + 4 + 5$, $14 - 12 - 1 + 11$.)*

31 Bird's eye view

Objectives
Level 3:
2D and 3D shapes;
views fron different
angles.

Organisation
Work with a group of
any size, or the whole
class.

Words to stress
names of shapes;
front, back, side,
top, bottom, opposite;
plan, elevation.

What you need
You need objects which children can look at from different
perspectives: for example, a cuboid box with different faces
(perhaps a box of cornflakes), a cylindrical tin, and something
like a toy bus or model house which is roughly cuboid in
shape.

What to do
Get the children to look carefully at the cornflake box. Ask:

- What shape is this face? And this one?
- Are they the same? How are they different?
- Where on the box is this face?
- Is there another face which is the same as this one? Where on the box is it?
- How many faces does this box have altogether?

Repeat the questions with the cylindrical tin. Then tell the children to imagine that they are little birds who can fly around and look at things from different directions. Ask:

- What would the bus look like if you looked down on it from the sky? What shape would you see?
- What if you looked at it from the front? From the back? From the side?
- What would your house look like if you flew above it? What would the school/church/park look like?

Four numbers

Objectives
Level 3:
number bonds to 20.

Organisation
Work with a group of any size, or the whole class.

Words to stress
plus, add, total, sum.

What you need
Choose any four different numbers from 1 to 10. Write them where everyone can see them.

What to do
Ask the children what totals they can make.

- What if you take the numbers two at a time? *(6 totals)*
- What if you double each number? *(4 totals)*
- What if you take the numbers in threes? *(4 totals)*
- What if you treble each number? *(4 totals)*
- What if you take all four numbers? *(1 total)*
- Are all the totals different?
- What if two of the numbers were the same?

Prisms

Objectives
Level 3:
2D and 3D shapes.

Organisation
Work with a group of
any size, or the whole
class.

Words to stress
names of shapes;
corner, face, edge.

What you need

You need a collection of prisms, and a board or wallchart on which to keep a record.

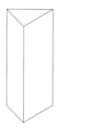  

What to do

Make sure that the children are familiar with the names of the prisms. Then put them away and ask them to imagine.

- Imagine a triangular prism. How many faces has it? How many corners? *(5 faces and 6 corners)*
- A cube is a square prism. How many faces has it? How many corners? *(6 faces and 8 corners)*
- Now think of a pentagonal prism. How many faces and corners does it have? *(7 faces and 10 corners)*
- What would be a good way to record our information?

Top face	Edges on top face	Number of faces	Number of corners
Triangle	3	5	6
Square	4	6	8
Pentagon	5	7	10

- How many faces do you think there will be on a hexagonal prism? *(8)* What about corners? *(12)*
- Can you see a pattern? *(The number of faces is going up one at a time; the number of corners is going up two at a time. The number of faces is two more than the number of sides; the number of corners is double the number of sides.)*
- Can you predict for heptagonal and octagonal prisms? *(9 faces and 14 corners, and 10 faces and 16 corners respectively)*
- What if the shape at the top of the prism had 20 sides? *(22 faces and 40 corners)*

You could extend this to the number of edges if appropriate.

Part 2b: More ideas for oral work

Most of the oral activities in this section are taken from *Talking Points*, by Anita Straker, published by Cambridge University Press (ISBN 0 521 44758 5). They are listed at each level of difficulty from 1 to 3. They cover number (including ordering numbers and place value, calculations, number patterns and data handling), and shape and space (including properties of shapes, simple line symmetry, position and direction, and measures). As in Part 2a, some of the activities are suitable for a whole class and others for small groups, and most will take about five minutes. Generally no writing or recording is required. Children should be encouraged to use their imaginations and mental skills as much as possible.

Number

Level 1	• *One, two, three...* How far can you count forwards? What about backwards? Count these cubes as I point slowly. Count as I point quickly. Count silently while I clap – first spaced evenly, then unevenly.
Level 1	• Close your eyes. Imagine a pattern made from five counters. Open your eyes and describe your pattern to your partner.
Level 1	• Imagine three big boxes on a table and three small cubes. Are there more boxes or more cubes? Let's set them out. Put a cube in each box. Are there fewer cubes or fewer boxes? Imagine putting the three cubes into one box. Are there the same number of cubes as boxes? Pile the boxes on top of each other. Guess how tall the tower will be. How many boxes are there now? Put the cubes in a tower as well. Are there more boxes than cubes? Hide all three of the cubes. How many cubes are hidden? Imagine three big apples. Would there be fewer apples, or fewer cubes? More apples or more boxes? 
Level 1	• Say a pattern of sounds: for example, tick, tick, tock, tick, tick, tock, tick, tick... Stop the pattern suddenly. Can you continue it? Try with musical instruments, or in PE with hop, jump, skip.

Level 1	• *First, second, third…* Look at this string of beads. Point to the third one. What colour is the sixth bead? What position is the second yellow bead? Which bead comes one before the third red bead? Two after the second green bead?

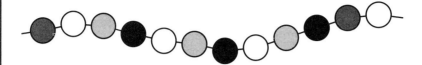

Level 1	• Can you point half way … along this table, down this chair, across this book, along the wall? Can you stand half way to the door? How could you find half of … this ribbon, lump of plasticine, piece of paper?
Level 1	• In PE, can you think of ways of finding half of the number in the class (for example, taking partners, or lining up in two matching lines)? Does everyone have a partner? How many pairs? Find a different partner. How many pairs now? What would happen if two children sat out?
Level 1	• Imagine a set of things that are red. What could be in it? What if we made a set of things that are not red? What about sets made of wood / not made of wood, bendy things / rigid things?

Level 1	• Play *Stand up, Sit down.*
	Stand up all the children who are wearing navy socks.
	Why isn't Sabina in the set? Why isn't Ben in the set?
	What can we call the set of children standing up? The set sitting down?
	Now try with:
	    all those who are wearing something green;
	    all those who are not six years old;
	    all those with blue eyes **and** with a younger sister;
	    all those wearing trousers **and** not wearing black shoes;
	    all those who came to school on a bus **or** in a car.

Level 1	• Imagine some flowers, or pieces of fabric, shapes, pebbles, letters of the alphabet, coins, flowers, greetings cards … How could we sort them?
Level 1	• What number is on your front door, on the bus which stops outside the school, on your telephone …? Where else have you seen a number?
Level 1	• How many buttons on your clothes? Who has most? Least? Two less than Winston? One more than Susie?
Level 1	• Imagine a large handful of straws. How many do you think there would be? How could we count them? How many do you think there would be in a handful of cubes? What about paper-clips? Think of some more things. How many would there be in a handful?

Levels 1, 2	• How old are you? How old were you last year? How old will you be two years from now? How old is your sister? Who is older, you or your sister? What is the difference in your ages?
Levels 1,2	• Whose clothes have the greatest number of colours? How many more colours has Sibani than Ruth? Who has fewer colours, Aziz or Sam?
Levels 1, 2	• How could you pay for a choc-bar costing 5p? Costing 8p?
Levels 1, 2	• Imagine 7 shells in a box. I take 3 out. How many are left in the box?
Levels 1, 2	• Play this game on your calculator. It's called One Hop to Five. I shall choose a number from 0 to 10 which you must put in your display. Now add or subtract just one number to make an answer of 5. Tomorrow we'll play One Hop to Seven. Next week we'll play Two hops to Five.
Levels 1, 2	• Can you think of ways of making patterns using playing cards? red, red, black, red, red, black... odd, even, odd, even... hearts, clubs, clubs, spades, hearts, clubs, clubs, spades, ...
Levels 1, 2	• Put these cards with numbers on in order. Now close your eyes while I change two cards around. Can you say which cards I changed over?
Levels 1, 2	• I put out these cards so that you could see them. Then I shuffled them up. I took one away secretly. Can you work out which one I took?
Levels 1, 2	• Close your eyes and imagine choosing two cards from a 1 to 9 pack. If you put them side by side, what is the biggest number you could make? What is the smallest number? What if you chose three cards?

Level 2	• Play *Too big, too small*. One person thinks of a number between 0 and 100. The others in the group try to guess what it is. The person who knows the number may only answer 'too big' or 'too small'. What is the least number of guesses you need? *(7)*
Level 2	• What numbers lie between 13 and 18? Between 23 and 28? Between 123 and 128? Can you think of a number between 4 and 5?
Level 2	• I am going to sing two notes: doh and me. Can you count the number of dohs? doh, doh, me, me, doh, doh, me, me, doh, doh, me, me, ... doh, doh, doh, me, me, doh, doh, doh, me, me, ... Now count the number of dohs and mes separately.
Level 2	• Imagine a set of dominoes. Which of them have a total of 1 spot, 2 spots, 3 spots, ..., 11 spots, 12 spots?
Level 2	• Five goals were scored in a football match. How many different final scores could there have been? *(6)* What if there were four goals, or six goals? How many different final scores then? *(5 or 7 respectively)*
Level 2	• These words all have something to do with numbers: *even, odd, double, twice, twin, couple, pair, half, halve, quarter, ...* Do you know what they mean?
Level 2	• How many children have some crisps in their lunch box? How many have fruit? Who has some chocolate? Who has a bread roll? Do more children have crisps than have fruit? How many more? Do fewer children have a bread roll than have chocolate? What is the difference between the number with a roll and the number with fruit?
Level 2	• These birds visited a bird table when we watched for 5 minutes.  Which kind of bird came twice? How many more sparrows than blue tits came? How many birds came altogether? Which birds didn't come? Which bird came most often? Can you think why?

Level 2 | • Today we are going to play Make 8. I shall hold up some of my fingers. Can you hold up enough of your fingers to make 8 altogether?

Level 2 | • Can you think of a set of coins that is worth 6p? Can you find any more? How many different sets can you think of altogether? *(6 sets)*

Level 2 | • Close your eyes and imagine a stick of two blue and two pink cubes. How could they be arranged?

2 + 2   **1 + 2 + 1**   **1 + 1 + 1 + 1**

Level 2 | • Imagine a stick of six cubes. The cubes are either red or yellow. How many of each colour could there be? *(6R, 5R and 1Y, 4R and 2Y, 3R and 3Y, 2R and 4Y, 1R and 5Y, 6Y)*

Level 2 | • Can you find …
a pair of even numbers with a total of 6? *(4 and 2)*
a pair of odd numbers which make 8 altogether? *(1 and 7 or 3 and 5)*
three odd numbers which add up to 9? *(1, 3 and 5)*
an odd number and an even number with a sum of 7? *(1,6 or 2,5 or 3,4)*

Level 2 | • How could you pay for a ball costing 20p with silver coins? *(4 × 5p, or 2 × 5p and 1 × 10p, or 2 × 10p or 1 × 20p)*

Level 2 | • What differences can you make from two of these numbers? *(1, 2, 3, 4, 5)*
What totals can you make? *(8, 10, 11, 12, 13, 15)*

3 5 7 8

Level 2 | • Imagine taking just three coins out of a purse. What amounts up to 10p might you take? *(3p, 4p, 5p, 6p, 7p, 8p, 9p)*

Level 2, 3 | • What pairs of numbers have a difference of 10?

Levels 2, 3 | • The answer is 10 (or any other number). What is the question?

Levels 2, 3 | • What is 36 + 10? 36 + 50? What is 26 – 10? 86 – 50?

Levels 2, 3	• What numbers could ■ and ▲ stand for if ■ + ▲ = 17? Is there a pattern?
Levels 2, 3	• Imagine having 8 straws. How many kisses (crosses) could you make? Imagine making 3 kisses. How many straws would you use? Now imagine having 9 straws. Could you use them all to make kisses? Try some more numbers. What numbers allow you to use all your straws to make kisses? *(Evens)* What if we imagined making triangles or squares?
Levels 2, 3	• My pack of 5 stamps contains only 2p and 5p stamps. What are the possible values of the pack? *(10p, 13p, 16p, 19p, 22p, 25p)*
Levels 2, 3	• Barat bought a soft drink from the machine. It cost 20p. The machine takes 2p, 5p and 10p. How could Barat pay for the drink? What possibilities are there? *(6 ways: 2 ×10p; 1 × 10p + 2 × 5p; 1 × 10p + 5 × 2p; 4 × 5p; 2 × 5p + 5 × 2p; 10 × 2p)*

Levels 2, 3	• *Units, tens, hundreds, thousands.* How far can you count in tens, or hundreds, or thousands? How do we say these numbers: 43, 107, 2006? Can you write sixty two in the air? Two thousand and seventeen?
Levels 2, 3	• Close your eyes and imagine the number four hundred and fifty two drawn in the air in front of you.. Which digit is on the left? Which is on the right? Change these two digits over. What does your number say now? What is the biggest number you could make with the digits? What is the smallest number you could make?
Levels 2, 3	• Everyone take a calculator. Put one hundred and three in your display. Show your partner. Are your displays the same? Now clear the display and put in two hundred and seventy. Now try one thousand and ninety three. Each time compare with your friends.

Level 3

- Can you describe this pattern? What would happen next?
  How many blobs? How many lines?

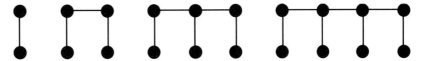

Level 3

- Suggest ways of making 50p using only 5p, 10p and 20p coins.
  How many different ways can you find? *(12 different ways)*

Level 3

- My microwave oven has buttons for 10 minutes, 1 minute, 10 seconds
  and 1 second. How do I get it to show 23 minutes? How do I get it to
  show 45 seconds?

Level 3

- I paid £1 exactly for some pencils. What might one pencil have cost, and
  how many did I get? *(For example, 10 at 10p, 20 at 5p, 5 at 20p, 50 at 2p ...)*

Level 3

- What is the cost of 10 crayons at 6p each? 100 crayons?
  How many pence in £1.27, in £1.05, in £1.50?
  If your calculator showed 1.5, how much money would this be? *(£1.50)*

Level 3

- How did you come to school today?
  What was the most common way?
  Will it be different tomorrow?
  What if ... no buses were running?
  　　　　　the weather were different?
  　　　　　there were twice as many children?
  What can you tell from comparing these two graphs?
  What do you think are the reasons for the differences?

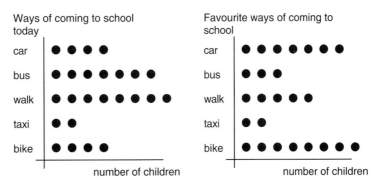

Level 3

- Can 7 be made as the sum of consecutive numbers? *(3 + 4)*
  What about 15? *(7 + 8)* Can you do it another way? *(4 + 5 + 6)*
  What other numbers between 1 and 20 are sums of consecutive numbers?

Level 3

- Estimate the number of shoelace holes in the class.

Shape and space

Level 1

- Do you have a favourite pattern? Can you describe it to me?

Level 1

- Imagine making a pattern of counters or cubes or beads in different colours and sizes. Can you describe it to me? How would it continue?

Level 1

- I've made this pattern from squares and circles, but I've secretly taken out one or two pieces and closed up the spaces. Which pieces do you think are missing?

Level 1

- In a PE session, can you sit or stand or lie: *next to/behind/in front of/beside/ at the side of* ... your partner? Who is sitting behind Manuel?
Can you make *long/short/fast/slow* steps or strides? Make *wide/narrow/ thick/thin* shapes.
Give instructions to move making use of words like: *up, down, left, right, forwards, backwards, towards, away from, over, under, through, across, along, clockwise, anticlockwise.*

Level 1

- Look round the classroom. What is *higher than, lower than, above, below, between, in the middle of, at the edge of, in the corner of,* ...?

Level 1

- Using a set of shapes (for example, felt shapes and felt board), can you:
put the red aeroplane *above* the boat;
put the van *below* the green aeroplane;
put the car *beside* the van?

Level 1

- This diagram shows eight children with coloured hats standing in a circle. They are facing inwards.

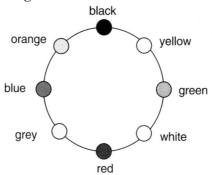

Which hat is to the left of the blue one? To the right of the black one?
To the left of the green one? To the right of the grey one?
What if they are facing outwards? Make up your own questions.

Level 1

- Build something with 10 cubes. Tell me about your model. How many cubes in Inderjit's tower, in Samuel's L-shape, in Mandy's box ... Whose model is the tallest/shortest/widest?

Level 1 | • Can you draw these shapes in the air for me: a triangle, a square, a circle? What about a straight line, a wavy line, a zig-zag line, a spiral?

Level 1 | • Stand opposite a partner. Move your arms, legs, head, and so on. Can your partner reflect your movements? If you move your left arm, which arm does your partner move? What if you stand side by side, and imagine a mirror placed between you?

Level 1 | • Tell me about something that is *heavy, light, long, short, thick, thin, wide, narrow, full, empty, hot, cold,* ... Or is *heavier, lighter, longer,* ...

Level 1 | • What day of the week is it? Which month is your birthday? What took place *today, yesterday, last month, long ago,* ...? What will take place *soon, tomorrow, next week, next year,* ...?

Level 1 | • Imagine things you can just manage to carry. Tell me about them. What things would be too heavy to carry?
Will this paper be enough to cover this book? How could you tell?
Will all these bricks fit into this box?

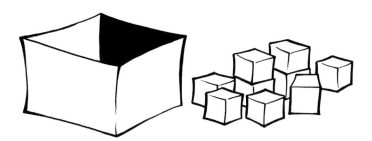

Level 1 | • Which do you think takes up more room, this box or this tin? How could we find out? What things would fit in this bucket? In this matchbox?

Level 1 | • Which car might roll further than this one? Why do you think so?

Level 1 | • What shape is inside this 'feely' bag? How do you know?

Level 1 | • First have a good look at this collection of shapes. Now shut your eyes. Listen carefully while I describe a shape to you... Now open your eyes. Can you pick up the shape I was describing?
Now can you describe one for someone else to guess?

Level 1	• Tell me some things that are very flat, very straight, very round, very twisty, very pointed …
Level 1	• Describe a butterfly for me.

Level 1	• Imagine a box. Can you describe it for me. What shape is its lid? What do its sides look like? What shape is its bottom? How tall is it?
Level 1	• Can you think of any shapes with no corners?
Level 1	• How much of this string would you need to measure all the way round this circle? Can you guess and then we'll try it.
Levels 1, 2	• If you were very tiny, and you were inside a matchbox, what would you see? What would you see if you were inside a thimble? What would you see if you were inside this empty packet of cornflakes?
Levels 1, 2	• What shapes are the faces of this cornflake packet? Are any the same?
Levels 1, 2	• If we cut down the edges of this box and opened it up, what shape do you think we would get?
Levels 1, 2	• If you ate a magic apple and were able to fly, what would you see if you flew over the school and looked down?
Levels 1, 2	• Imagine taking footsteps all the way round the outside of the rim of this hoop. How many do you think it would be? Guess and then try. Now guess how many footsteps it would be all the way round the inside of the rim.
Levels 1, 2	• How many children could sit on one sheet of newspaper on the floor? How many could sit inside this hoop?
Levels 1, 2	• How many sheets of newspaper will it take to cover the painting table?
Levels 1, 2	• Can you make a lump of plasticine to drop into this jar of water? You must do it so that the level of the water rises just to this mark.

Level 2
- Where could you see a *dome, spire, cone, pyramid, sphere, cube, cylinder, prism, ...?* What about *circles, triangles, rectangles, ...?*

Level 2
- When do we use the word *tall*, and when do we use *high*?
  When do we use *length*, and when do we use *distance*?
  When do we use *capacity*, and when do we use *volume*?

Level 2
- What words do you know that help to describe lines? For example, *straight, wavy, rippled, rays, curved, spiral, zig-zag, criss-cross, broad, narrow, jagged, smooth, dotted, dashed , horizontal, vertical, diagonal, ...* Can you see any of these in the classroom? Do you know any places outside where you can see them?

Level 2
- Where can you see patterns of shapes around the school? (*For example, on clothes, in a brick wall, in paving, on a fence, in wall tiles, ...*) Can you describe the different patterns?

Level 2
- Look around the classroom. Can you see any right angles? What shapes have only right angles in them? Which have no right angles?

Level 2
- Can you describe how to get from the classroom to the hall?

Level 2
- Is it further from the school to the mosque, from the school to the station, or the school to the High Street? Why do you think so?

Level 2
- A turtle is at the black peg, facing up the page.
  It moves LEFT 90, FORWARD 3, LEFT 90, FORWARD 3.
  Where does it get to?

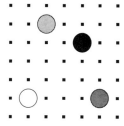

Now make up some more problems.

Level 2	• Tell me about things that turn: for example, the hands of a clock, taps, see-saws, doors, lids of jars, pages of a book, the sails of a windmill, a helicopter rotor, swings, scissors, steering wheels, … Which turn about a point and which about a line?
Level 2	• How long do you think this ribbon is? What about this one?
Level 2	• Estimate how many hand spans you can reach, step, jump, … What about your friend? How much further can one of you reach, step, jump, …?
Level 2	• What questions might have the answer: a width of six straws, a weight of five conkers, a capacity of four cups?
Level 2	• What is the least number of cubes needed to complete:

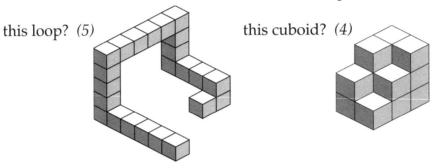

this loop? *(5)*   this cuboid? *(4)*

Level 2	• Tell me about some things that hold about half a litre. What things hold less than half a litre? What things hold more than half a litre?
Level 2	• Two children each drank half a litre of lemonade. How much did they drink altogether? Brian picked 9 kg of apples and May picked 4 kg. How many more kilograms of apples did Brian pick? How many times can I cut 4 cm from this 9 cm ribbon?
Level 2	• Afzhal balanced a ball with 45 shells. Parveen balanced the same ball with 50 shells. Can you explain why?
Level 2	• It's 10 o'clock now. How many more hours until 3 o'clock? In three days time I'm going to the dentist. What day will that be? What date will that be?
Level 2	• What time will it be when we: eat lunch, use the hall for PE, do mental maths, watch TV, have assembly, …? How long do you think it will take for everyone to get changed, to read a page of this book, to sing a hymn, …?

Levels 2, 3	• Could an elephant walk through the door of the classroom? What would we need to know about the door? What would we need to know about the elephant?

Levels 2, 3	• How tall are you? How tall are you if you stand on a chair?
Levels 2, 3	• Here are two different containers. What questions could you ask about them?
Levels 2, 3	• Imagine putting two red panes of glass in a 2 × 2 window. Tell me what it would look like.

Levels 2, 3	• What words do you know that describe patterns? For example, *striped, checked, spotty, polka dot, plaid, criss-cross, scalloped, repeated, random, regular, half-drop, symmetrical, …* What kinds of patterns do you see on clothes?
Level 3	• Look at these two leaves. Which has the longer perimeter? Which has the larger area? Why do you think so?

Level 3	• Could a sponge weigh more than a marble? *(It might if it were wet.)*
Level 3	• Can you estimate one minute while I look at the stop watch? Start when I say 'Go'. Tell me when to stop. What events last about one minute? 20 minutes? One hour?

Level 3	• How could you find out the volume of your hand? How could you find out the capacity of your hand?
Level 3	• How many things can you think of that weigh about 5kg? What things are about 10cm long/tall/wide/deep? 10 metres?
Level 3	• What units do you know? What are they used to measure?
Level 3	• Why is it important to have equal (standard) units?
Level 3	• Here is a picture of Monty. Without showing the picture, tell your partner how to make him.

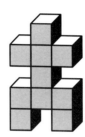

If you made the smallest archway to fit round Monty, how many cubes wide would it be? *(5 cubes wide)* How many cubes tall? *(6 cubes tall)* How many cubes would you need altogether for the archway? *(15)*

Level 3	• Imagine a square. Fold it in half. What shape is it now? Imagine folding it in half again. What shape is it now?
Level 3	• The triangle is half a shape. Describe the whole shapes you could make.

Level 3	• Describe some capital letters that are symmetrical. Draw them in the air.
Level 3	• Play Noughts and Crosses with a difference. Take turns to tell the other player where to put a mark.
Level 3	• Describe the patterns you could make by putting two tiles like one of these side by side, or one above the other, or four of them in a square.

Part 3: Puzzles and games

These activities are intended for children to work on by themselves, at school or at home, though it is likely that some children will need some initial help with reading the instructions in order to get started.

Most of the activities will take from 10 to 15 minutes, assuming that games are played several times. The games are for two or more children to play together; some are games of chance and others require a simple strategy. The puzzles are for individual children, several of the puzzle sheets can be used more than once because children choose the numbers that they start with. The notes on pages 72 to 74 give details of the level of difficulty and the skills or strategies needed, with solutions to the puzzles.

The games and puzzles provide another way of helping children to practise quick recall of number facts and mental arithmetic skills. They also allow you to assess children's progress by observing what they do and listening to what they say.

Where it is appropriate you could ask children:

- What's the best way to start?
- Where could you be after one, two, three, … moves?
- How could you record your moves?
- What is the least number of moves you need to win the game or solve the puzzle?
- Who do you think will win? Now play and see if you were right.
- Could you write about ways of winning?
- Could you change the rules slightly to make another game or puzzle?

As children do the activities you might look for:

- growing confidence as indicated by questions like: 'Shall I try … ?' compared with 'What shall I do now?';
- the speed and accuracy of their recall;
- whether they are resorting to counting on their fingers;
- their ability to talk clearly about what they have been doing, to you or to their friends, or to write about or record their work in some way;
- whether they give up easily or persevere;
- how cooperatively they work with others.

Finish the pattern.

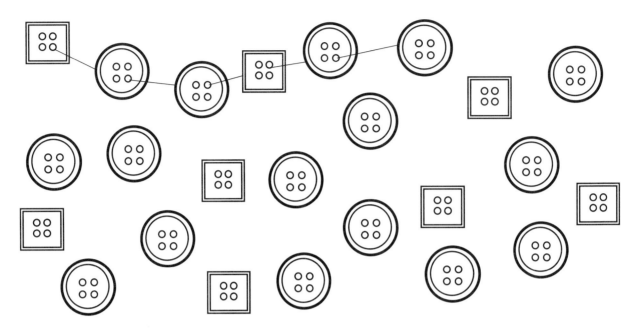

Make a pattern.

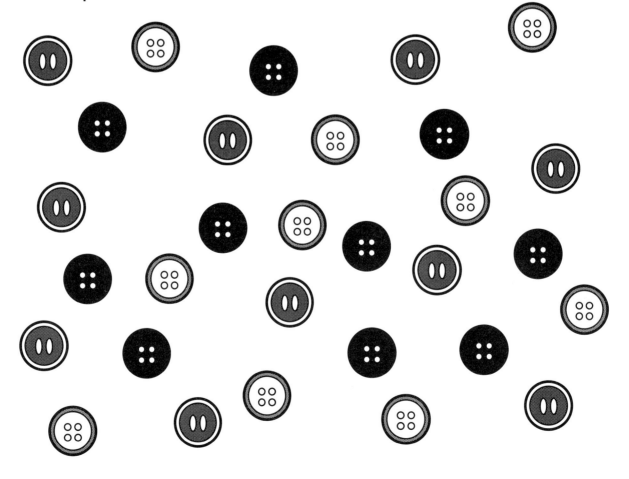

From *Mental Maths* Anita Straker © Cambridge University Press 1996

2 Rugs

Complete a pattern on this rug.
Colour it.

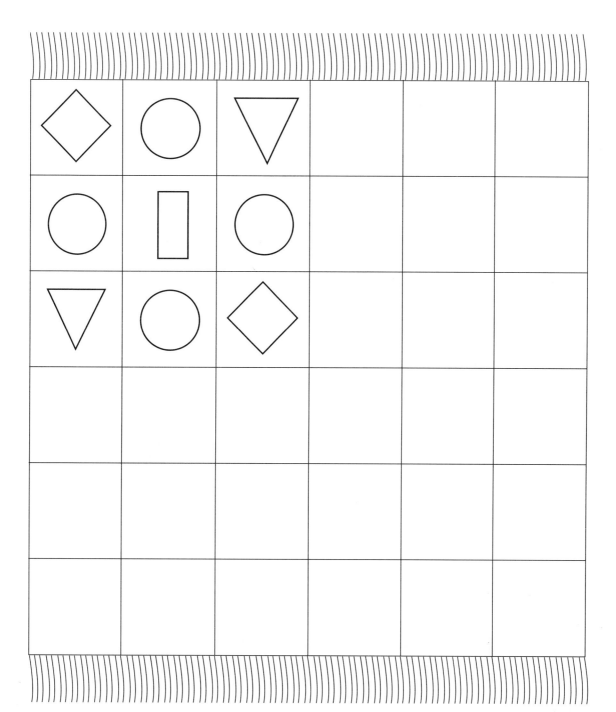

How many: squares? ☐ rectangles? ☐

circles? ☐ triangles? ☐

If you put 6 spots in 3 boxes, how many in each box?
Investigate. Draw some spots in each box.

Now try 7 spots.

From *Mental Maths* Anita Straker © Cambridge University Press 1996

Name:

Use only these.

2 3 5 + −

Complete these. You can use the same number twice.

1 = ☐ ☐ ☐

2 = ☐ ☐ ☐

3 = ☐ ☐ ☐

4 = ☐ ☐ ☐

5 = ☐ ☐ ☐

6 = ☐ ☐ ☐

7 = ☐ ☐ ☐

8 = ☐ ☐ ☐

From *Mental Maths* Anita Straker © Cambridge University Press 1996

Name:

Choose a number from 10 to 20.
Write it in the middle circle.

Make three different patterns to go backwards and
forwards from your number.

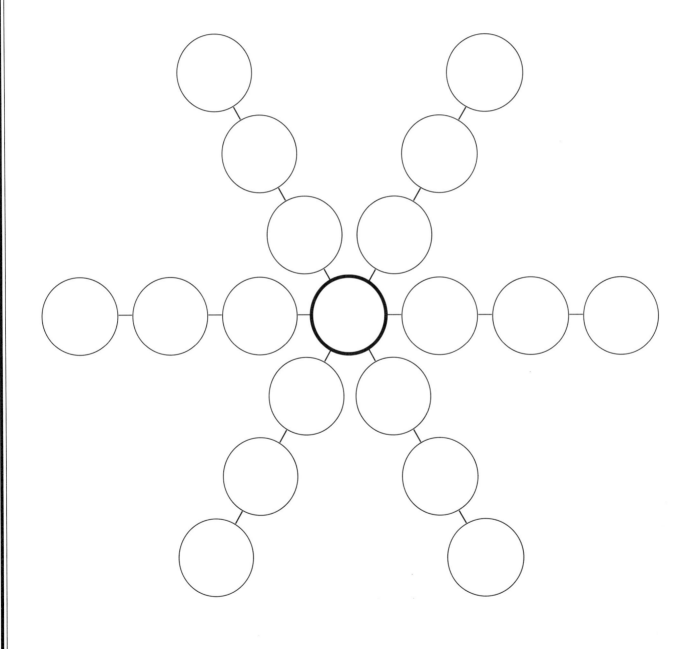

From *Mental Maths* Anita Straker © Cambridge University Press 1996

Name:

You need pens in three colours.
Colour each circle in a different colour.

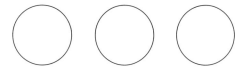

Now use all three colours in a different order.

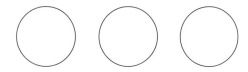

Make as many different patterns as you can.
Use all three colours each time.

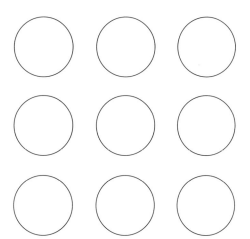

Draw more circles if you need to.

How many different patterns did you find?

What could you try next?

Name:

1

	D	E	F
A	3	1	2
B	2	4	3
C	1	3	1

Which row has the biggest total? ☐

Which column has the biggest total? ☐

2 Write a number from 1 to 5 in each box.

	D	E	F
A			
B			
C			

Which row has the biggest total? ☐

Which column has the biggest total? ☐

From *Mental Maths* Anita Straker © Cambridge University Press 1996

Name:

Write 3 different numbers
in the circles to add up to
the one in the middle.

1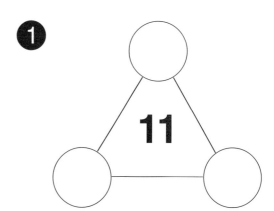

2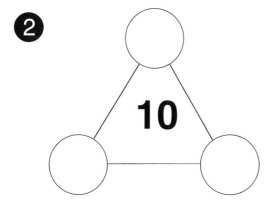

3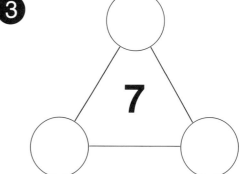

Write your own number in the middle.

4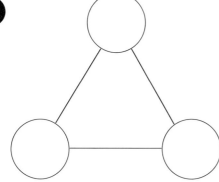

5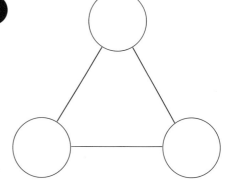

From *Mental Maths* Anita Straker © Cambridge University Press 1996

Name:

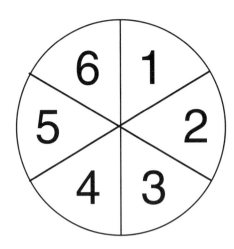

Use the numbers 1 to 6 only.
You can use each number as often as you like.

Write a total to aim for: either 10, 11 or 12.

Investigate different ways of making your total.

$\square + \square + \square$ $\square + \square + \square$

$\square + \square + \square$ $\square + \square + \square$

$\square + \square + \square$ $\square + \square + \square$

Write any more ways here.

From *Mental Maths* Anita Straker © Cambridge University Press 1996

Name:

In this grid: every row has a counter of each colour;
        every column has a counter of each colour.

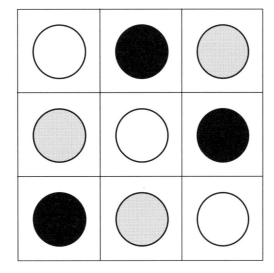

Use 4 red, 4 yellow, 4 blue and 4 green counters.
Arrange them on this grid.
Each row and column must have a counter of each colour.
Write the colours in the boxes.

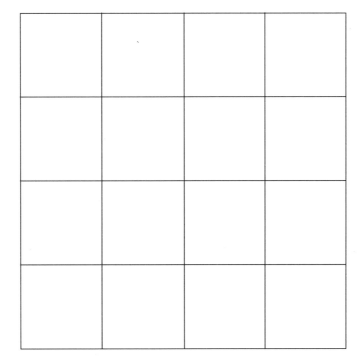

(11) Counters

Name:

Use 15 counters each time.
Write how many counters you used in each box.

1 Make each box 1 more than the one before.

☐ ☐ ☐ ☐ ☐

2 Make each box double the one before.

☐ ☐ ☐ ☐

3 Make each box 3 more than the one before.

☐ ☐ ☐

4 Make each box hold either 2 or 3 counters.

☐ ☐ ☐ ☐ ☐ ☐

From *Mental Maths* Anita Straker © Cambridge University Press 1996

12 Sums

Name:

1 Use only these numbers.

6   1   4   10

Write a number in each box to make each sum correct.

☐	+	☐	=	7	☐	−	☐	=	6
☐	+	☐	=	14	☐	−	☐	=	5
☐	+	☐	=	10	☐	−	☐	=	3
☐	+	☐	=	5	☐	−	☐	=	2

2 Write a number from 1 to 10 in each circle.

◯ ◯ ◯ ◯

Use your numbers to make up some sums.
Use a different pair each time.

☐	+	☐	=	☐	☐	−	☐	=	☐
☐	+	☐	=	☐	☐	−	☐	=	☐
☐	+	☐	=	☐	☐	−	☐	=	☐

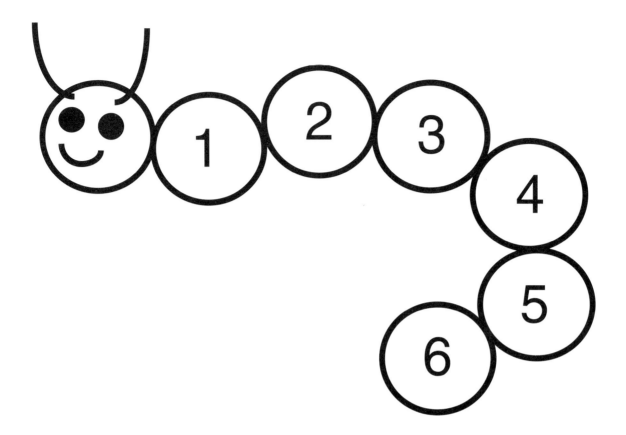

Rules

You need a dice.
Each player needs 6 counters in their own colour.

Take turns to roll the dice.
If you can, cover a number with a counter.
The numbers must be covered in order from 1 to 6.

The winner is the one who has covered most numbers
when all the circles are full.

For a change, start at 6 instead of 1.

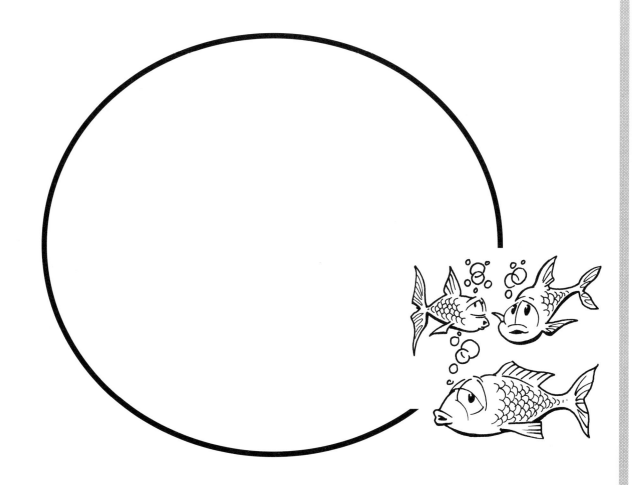

2 Fish pond

Rules

You need a pile of counters to use as fish.

Take turns to put **either** one **or** two fish into the pond.

The player who puts in enough fish to make a total of 10 in the pond wins the game.

For a change, take turns to put **either** one **or** two **or** three fish into the pond.

Rules

You need different coloured counters (nails) for each player, and a coin.

In turn, choose any number from 1 to 10 and say it. Toss the coin.

For heads, put a nail on the number that is one more. For tails, put a nail on the number that is one less.

If the number is already nailed, you miss a turn.

The winner is the one with most nails on the horseshoe when all the numbers are nailed.

From *Mental Maths* Anita Straker © Cambridge University Press 1996

| 10 |
| 9 |
| 8 |
| 7 |
| 6 |
| 5 |
| 4 |
| 3 |
| 2 |
| 1 |

Rules

You need a dice.
Put a big counter on
each cat.
Put a small counter
(mouse) by each hole.

Take turns.
Roll the dice.
Take that number of
steps up your path.
To catch the mouse you
must land exactly
on 10.

Next turn,
take the mouse and
start to come back.
You must land exactly
on the cat.

The winner is the first to
get the mouse to the cat.

| 10 |
| 9 |
| 8 |
| 7 |
| 6 |
| 5 |
| 4 |
| 3 |
| 2 |
| 1 |

$\boxed{5}$ Five pence

For two players

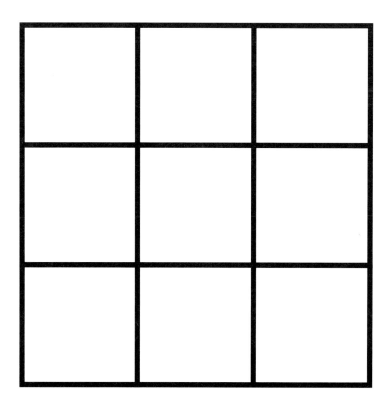

Rules

You need five 2p and five 1p coins,
and pencil and paper to keep the score.

In turn, choose a coin and put it on the grid.
If you make a line of three coins totalling 5p you score a point.

The winner is the one with most points when each square
has a coin in it.

For a change, try to make lines of 4p.

From *Mental Maths* Anita Straker © Cambridge University Press 1996

Make 12   For two or three players

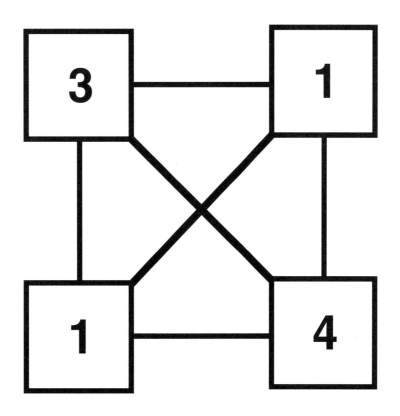

Rules

You need a counter.

One player puts the counter on a number and says it.

Take turns to slide the counter to another number.
Add on that number and say the new total.

The winner is the player to reach exactly 12.
If you go over 12 you lose.

For a change, choose a different total to aim for.

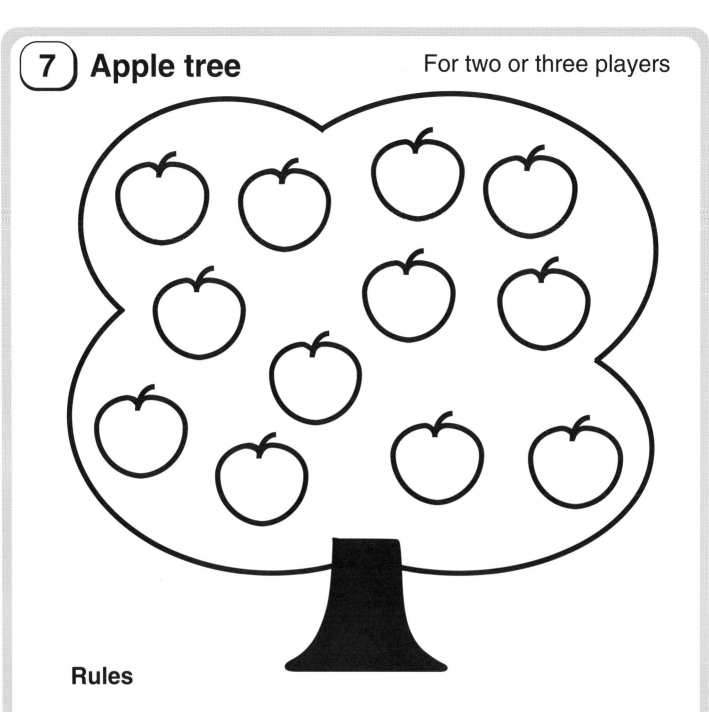

Rules

You need 2 dice.
Each player needs some counters in their own colour.

Take turns to roll both dice.
If the total is 7, cover an apple with a counter.

The winner is the one with most apples
when they are all covered.

For a change, make the total 6 or 8.

From *Mental Maths* Anita Straker © Cambridge University Press 1996

Rules

You need a calculator and some small counters.
Use one side of the ladybird each.

Take turns to enter a number from 1 to 10 in the display.

Pass the calculator to the other player,
who must add a number to make a total of 10.
If correct, that player covers a spot with a counter.

The winner is the first to cover all their spots.

For a change, choose a different total.

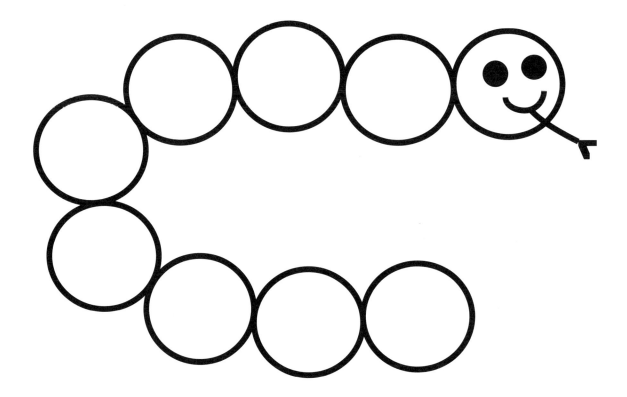

Rules

You need 2 different coloured pens, one for each player, and 2 dice.

Take turns to roll both dice.
Write the total number in a circle.
A number can only be written once.
The numbers in all the circles must be in order.

If there is no space for a number you miss a turn.

The player who has written most numbers when all the circles are full wins the game.

From *Mental Maths* Anita Straker © Cambridge University Press 1996

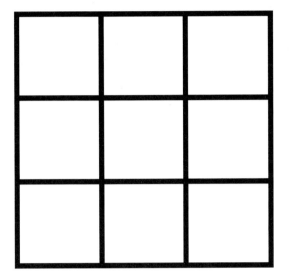 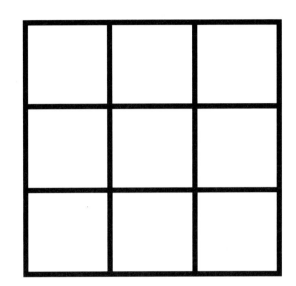

Rules

You need a pencil and a dice.
Use one grid each.

Take turns to roll the dice.
Double the number rolled.
Write it in any box on your grid.
Carry on until each grid is full.

Now take turns to roll the dice again.
If you can, cross out the double of the number.

The winner is the first to cross out all their numbers.

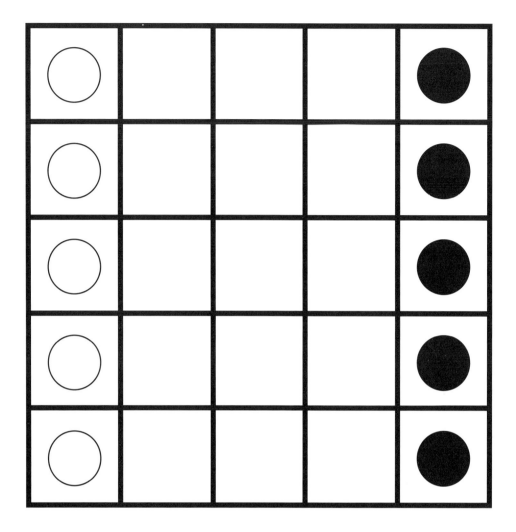

Rules

Put 5 counters of your own colour on the circles.

Take turns to move one of your own counters horizontally one space at a time.

When two counters are next to each other, the player whose turn it is can jump over the other counter.

The winner is the first to get all their counters to the other side.

From *Mental Maths* Anita Straker © Cambridge University Press 1996

12 Tracks

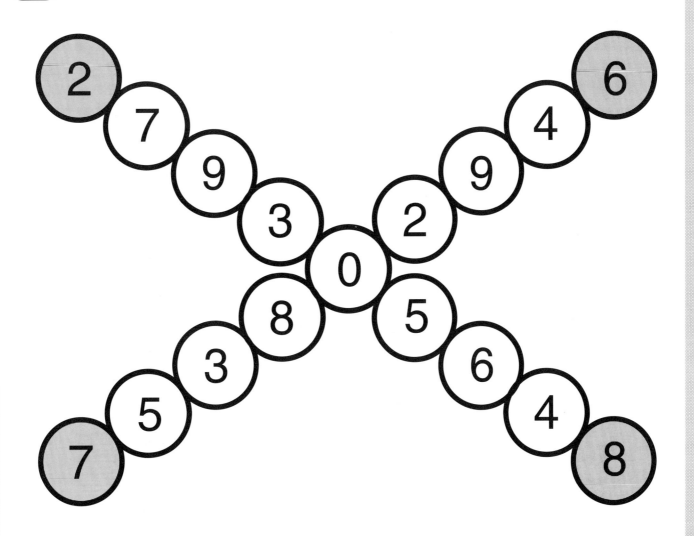

Rules

You need a counter and a calculator for each player.
Each player puts a counter on any grey circle.

In turn, players say how to get from their number
to the next one. The other player checks on the calculator.

Only if the statement is correct is the counter moved on.

The winner is the first to reach any other grey circle.

Notes on the puzzles and games

The puzzles

Level 1

1	Buttons	Repeating patterns.

The first set of beads should continue to be threaded by shape: one square, two circular. There are various routes to follow, but by spiralling around the edge towards the centre the thread does not cross over itself.

The second set can be threaded according to children's own criteria: perhaps by the number of holes (two or four), by colour (grey, black or white), or by rim (rim, no rim).

2 Rugs

Repeating patterns; line symmetry.

The pattern can be completed by continuing each row across the rug, and each column down. Alternatively, children may decide to reflect the pattern about a vertical line, and/or a horizontal line, through the centre of the rug.

3 Spots

Addition to 6.

With 6 spots: $1 + 1 + 4$ $\quad$ $1 + 2 + 3$ $\quad$ $2 + 2 + 2$

With 7 spots: $1 + 1 + 5$ $\quad$ $1 + 2 + 4$ $\quad$ $1 + 3 + 3$ $\quad$ $2 + 2 + 3$

In this investigation, children may need to be reminded that the order of the numbers does not affect the total. More variations are possible if 0 is allowed.

4 Target

Addition or subtraction of 2, 3 and 5 to total up to 10.

$1 = 3 - 2$ $\quad$ $2 = 5 - 3$ $\quad$ $3 = 5 - 2$ $\quad$ $4 = 2 + 2$ $\quad$ $5 = 2 + 3$ $\quad$ $6 = 3 + 3$

$7 = 2 + 5$ $\quad$ $8 = 3 + 5$

Children may need to be reminded that the order of the numbers for addition makes no difference to the total, whereas with subtraction the order matters.

Level 2

5 Snowflake

Addition and subtraction patterns.

Children will choose there own patterns: for example, sequences with a difference of 1, 2, 3, 5 or 10.

6 3 colours

Patterns created by the different arrangements of three colours.

In this investigation, the order of the colours in any row of three is significant. If the three colours are red, blue and pink then the six arrangements are:

red blue pink $\quad$ blue red pink $\quad$ pink blue red

red pink blue $\quad$ blue pink red $\quad$ pink red blue

If 4 circles are coloured in 4 different colours, there are 24 arrangements. If a colour can be used more than once, there are 27 arrangements of 3 colours.

7 **Totals** Addition of three digits from 1 to 5.
Row B has the biggest total of 9.
Column E has the biggest total of 8.
Children can continue to make up more problems like this on squared paper.

8 **Triangles** Addition of three numbers to total up to 11.
Accept any answer where three different numbers have the correct total.
The larger the total, the greater the number of possibilities.
For 7, there is only one possibility: 1, 2, 4.
For 8, the two possibilities are 1,2,5 or 1,3,4.
For 9, the three possibilities are: 1,2,6 or 1,3,5 or 2,3,4.
For 10, the four possibilities are: 1,2,7 or 1,3,6 or 1,4,5 or 2,3,5.
For 11, the five possibilities are: 1,2,8 or 1,3,7 or 1,4,6 or 2,3,6 or 2,4,5.

Level 3

9 **One to six** Addition of three digits from 1 to 6 to total 10, 11 or 12.
The possible combinations using 3 digits (with repeats) are:

for 10	1,3,6	1,4,5	2,2,6	2,3,5	2,4,4	3,3,4
for 11	1,4,6	2,3,6	2,4,5	3,3,5	3,4,4	5,5,1
for 12	1,5,6	2,4,6	2,5,5	3,3,6	3,4,5	5,5,2	4,4,4

Using 2 digits, there are a few more possibilities.
For 10 there is 4,6 or 5,5. For 11 there is 5,6. For 12 there is 6,6.

If the investigation is extended to 4 digits, there are more possibilities:

for 10	1,1,2,6	1,1,3,5	1,1,4,4	1,2,2,5	1,2,3,4	1,3,3,3	2,2,2,4
	2,2,3,3						
for 11	1,1,3,6	1,1,4,5	1,2,2,6	1,2,3,5	1,2,4,4	1,3,3,4	2,2,2,5
	2,2,3,4	2,3,3,3					
for 12	1,1,4,6	1,1,5,5	1,2,3,6	1,2,4,5	1,3,3,5	1,3,4,4	2,2,2,6
	2,2,3,5	2,2,4,4	2,3,3,4	3,3,3,3			

10 **4 colours** Patterns in a 4 × 4 square.
You will need to check that the counters
are arranged so that each row and column
has a counter of each colour.
Here is one possible solution.

R	Y	B	G
G	R	Y	B
B	G	R	Y
Y	B	G	R

11 **Counters** Number bonds, doubling, differences.

One more than the one before

| 1 | 2 | 3 | 4 | 5 |

Double the one before

| 1 | 2 | 4 | 8 |

3 more than the one before

| 2 | 5 | 8 |

Each holds 2 or 3 counters

| 2 | 2 | 2 | 3 | 3 | 3 |

12 **Sums** Sums and differences of pairs of numbers up to 20.

1 + 6 = 7	10 + 4 = 14	4 + 6 = 10	1 + 4 = 5
10 − 4 = 6	6 − 1 = 5	4 − 1 = 3	6 − 4 = 2

The games

1   Caterpillar

Ordering of numbers 1 to 6.
This is a game of chance which requires children to focus on the order of numbers 1 to 6. To find out who wins, a comparison must be made between pairs such as 3,3 or 4,2 or 5,1 or 6,0 to decide which number is greater.

2   Fish pond

Counting to 10; addition of 1 or 2 up to a total of 10.
There is a winning strategy, though children are likely to play at random at first. The player who is on 7 forces a win, since the other player can then only add 1 or 2 fish; this allows the player on 7 to add 2 or 1 fish to bring the total to 10. Similarly, 4 and 1 are winning positions. If there are two players only, the first can always win by adding one fish to the pond. When up to 3 fish can be added, the winning positions are 2 and 6. Take turns to go first.

3   More or less

One more or one less, within the range 1 to 10.
This is a simple strategic game. Players must consider carefully which number to choose; one with a space on either side is a better choice than one with an adjacent counter. To start, 1 and 10 are not as good as other numbers.

4   Mouse hole

Counting on to a total of 6.
A game of chance.

5   Five pence

Addition of 1p and 2p to total 5p.
A game of strategy in which the aim is to complete lines by placing 2p, 2p and 1p in them. 2p placed in the centre maximises chances of scoring.

Level 2

6   Make 12

Addition of 1, 3 or 4 up to a total of 12.
With two players, winning positions are 7 on 3, 8 on 4, 10 on 1.

7   Apple tree

Number bonds from 2 to 12.
A game of chance.

8   Ladybird

Counting on to a total of 10.
A game of chance.

9   Snake

Number bonds to 12; ordering of numbers 2 to 12.
Some strategy is required in the placing of numbers.

10   Doubles

Doubles of 1 to 6; halves of even numbers from 2 to 12.
A game of chance.

11   Jump

Using and applying maths to analyse moves in a logical game.
The best strategy is to keep one blank square between your counter and your opponent's in any row. The first player will always lose if the second reflects all his/her initial moves from the edge. Take turns to go first.

12   Tracks

Addition and subtraction in the range 0 to 9.
This game requires accurate recall of number bonds.

Answers: *Mental Maths Starter Book*

Mental Maths Starter Book is a separate booklet for six- and seven-year-olds to use. It involves addition and subtraction facts to 5, then to 10, then to 20. This extends to sums like 14 + 10 or 20 + 3 and differences such as 24 – 10 or 30 – 2. Multiplication and division by 2, 3, 4 or 5 in the range 0 to 20, and by 10 up to 10 × 10, are included. Questions cover ordinal numbers and introduce place value of tens and units. Odd and even numbers to 20, and simple fractions, are touched upon, as are days of the week, use of coins to 20p, and recognition of simple 2D shapes. Answers to the questions are given below.

Task 1a
1   4
2   4
3   3
4   3
5   5
6   3
7   2
8   6

Task 1b
1   6 is more
2   2p and 1p
3   5
4   One half
5   4 socks
6   D
7   4p
8   A rectangle

Task 1c

3 1 4 2

or its reflection

2 4 1 3

Task 1d
1   4
2   6
3   2
4   3
5   1
6   3
7   10
8   9

Task 2a
1   2
2   L
3   5
4   A circle
5   2 is less
6   3
7   4
8   3 toffees

Task 2b
1   2
2   4
3   1
4   4
5   2
6   3
7   3
8   1

Task 2c
1   2
2   6
3   2
4   5
5   5
6   8
7   7
8   4

Task 2d

2	4		1
2			5
3		3	1

Task 3a
1   Friday
2   3 sides
3   5
4   2 chews
5   5 is odd
6   5
7   7
8   2, 3, 5, 7.

Task 3b

	¹T		²T	E	³N
			W	H	I
⁴F	O	U	R		N
				E	E
⁵S	E	V	E	N	

Task 3c
1   2
2   2p and 2p
3   2
4   1 bird
5   N
6   8 is even
7   5p
8   One half

Task 3d

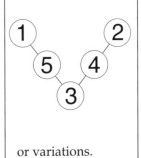

or variations.

Task 4a

1 1
2 6
3 1
4 3
5 5
6 3
7 6
8 4

Task 4b

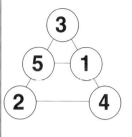

Task 4c

1 5
2 2
3 4
4 2
5 5
6 0
7 6
8 4

Task 4d

1 Blacky
2 Star
3 Amber
4 Star
5 Amber
6 Jess
7 Star
8 Amber

Task 5a

1 8
2 6
3 5
4 1
5 5
6 3
7 4
8 7

Task 5b

1 1
2 7p
3 W
4 One quarter
5 8 legs
6 Monday
7 3p
8 3 cherries

Task 5c

Greatest total is 9,
or 2 + 3 + 4, in the
bottom row.

Least total is 5,
or 2 + 1 + 2, in the
diagonal from top
right to bottom left.

Task 5d

1 6
2 2
3 4
4 2
5 16
6 20
7 3
8 6

Task 6a

1 5p and 1p
2 14 is greater
3 2
4 A triangle
5 5
6 2 and 4
7 4 corners
8 9 fish

Task 6b

1 12
2 6
3 10
4 7
5 7
6 12
7 20
8 2

Task 6c

2 5 3   6 4

Each ring has a
total of 10, half
the sum of all the
numbers.

Task 6d

1 11
2 16
3 6
4 11
5 8
6 3
7 1
8 13

Task 7a

1 5
2 50
3 5
4 12
5 8
6 0
7 14
8 4

Task 7b

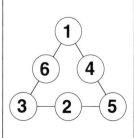

Task 7c

1 15
2 15
3 6
4 8
5 10
6 9
7 10
8 50

Task 7d

1 6
2 21
3 4kg
4 4 years old
5 2
6 11
7 3 boxes
8 A square

Task 8a

Eight possibilities:

2kg
3kg
4kg
5kg
6kg
7kg
8kg
10kg

Task 8b

1   2 and 6
2   30
3   2
4   12 is even
5   12 shoes
6   19
7   7 days
8   5

Task 8c

1   3
2   Tuesday
3   4 sides
4   11p
5   18
6   5p and 2p
7   3 boxes
8   3 rectangles

Task 8d

For 11: 4 sets
1   1   9
1   3   7
1   5   5
3   3   5
To extend, try
13: 5 sets
15: 8 sets

Task 9a

1   $6 \times 1p$ 6p
2   $3 \times 2p$ 6p
3   $7 \times 5p$ 35p
4   $4 \times 10p$ 40p
5   $5 \times 20p$ £1

Task 9b

1   0
2   1
3   16
4   10
5   30
6   4
7   14
8   16

Task 9c

	4		7	8
13	14	15	16	17
	24	25	26	
		35		

Task 9d

1   7
2   14
3   10
4   4
5   46
6   17
7   3
8   8

Task 10a

1   2
2   2
3   2
4   12
5   9
6   9
7   6
8   16

Task 10b

7	3	2
3	6	4
3	1	6

Task 10c

1   2
2   20
3   22
4   6
5   4
6   10
7   14
8   2

Task 10d

1   19p
2   10
3   2p, 2p and 1p
4   3 triangles
5   10
6   Tuesday
7   15
8   12 legs

Task 11a

1   50
2   12 is less
3   7 and 3
4   One half
5   Five 10p coins
6   7 is half way
7   5 cakes
8   A hexagon

Task 11b

1   6
2   20
3   7
4   2
5   18
6   8
7   6
8   15

Task 11c

1   40
2   9
3   10
4   12
5   12
6   8
7   19
8   7

Task 11d

5 ways

1	4		2	3
6	2		5	3

3	2		4	1
4	4		3	5

5	0
2	6

Task 12a

They should each carry 10 kg (half the total of all 6 bags).

(8 + 2) kg and
(4 + 3 + 2 + 1) kg

Task 12b

1　32 is greater
2　Nearer to 5
3　8 corners
4　Four 5p coins
5　11
6　14 eyes
7　2 tens
8　4

Task 12c

1　1 ten
2　8, 23, 27, 41
3　15 is odd
4　5 squares
5　15 dots
6　20p and 20p
7　6
8　3p

Task 12d

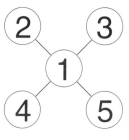

Task 13a

1　AN = 7
2　IT = 7
3　GAG = 5
4　NAN = 11
5　TIN = 11
6　ANT = 12
7　INN = 10
8　GAIN = 10

Task 13b

1　10
2　28
3　16
4　5
5　10
6　3
7　18
8　30

Task 13c

Next number: 10
The next: 12
And the next: 14

The pattern is even numbers so the 10th number is 20. 20th number is 40.

Task 13d

1　9
2　4
3　20
4　14
5　24
6　3
7　3
8　20

Task 14a

1　1
2　50
3　100
4　60
5　7
6　11
7　7
8　16

Task 14b

1　3
2　50p, 20p, 10p
3　One quarter
4　16 legs
5　Nearer to 10
6　13
7　4 tens
8　8 triangles

Task 14c

9 patterns
cloud, cloud
cloud, sun
cloud, rain
sun, sun
sun, cloud
sun, rain
rain, rain
rain, cloud
rain, sun

Task 14d

1　11
2　12
3　4
4　18
5　39
6　9
7　3
8　60

Task 15a

1　8p
2　10p, 2p, 2p, 1p
3　20
4　An octagon
5　Wednesday
6　Nearer to 20
7　14p
8　14 cakes

Task 15b

1　13
2　17
3　3
4　18
5　5
6　2
7　9
8　12

Task 15c

There are 7 different solutions, plus 7 reflections.

1 3 5 2 4
1 4 2 5 3
2 4 1 3 5
2 4 1 5 3
2 5 3 1 4
3 1 4 2 5
3 1 5 2 4

Task 15d

1　4
2　9
3　16
4　11
5　17
6　5
7　2
8　4